EXPLORATIONS IN ASSEMBLY
WITH CHILDREN

20p

Skipper

EXPLORATIONS IN ASSEMBLY WITH CHILDREN

by
DOROTHY J. TAYLOR

Suggestions for Assembly
in the Junior School

LUTTERWORTH EDUCATIONAL · GUILDFORD & LONDON

First published 1973

Second impression 1978

ISBN 0 7188 2042 8

Printed in Great Britain
by Ebenezer Baylis and Son Ltd.
The Trinity Press, Worcester, and London

Contents

Acknowledgements

GRATEFUL acknowledgement is made to the following authors and publishers for permission to quote copyright material, as well as to individuals who have given information and help.

The Bodley Head, for references relating to *The Boy Who Was Afraid* by Armstrong Sperry and *More Stories to Read and to Tell* by Norah Montgomerie.
The British and Foreign Bible Society for the story of James Evans and the Cree Bible from their leaflet, *The Birch Bark Talks*.
The Education Department of Christian Aid for the story of Cyrus Gaikwad from the leaflet *Friends in Action*, no. 3.
Miss Doris Gill for lines from her hymn, *Come let us remember the joys of the town*.
The Guardian Newspapers for the reference to Chris Cornell from the issue of August 21, 1972.
The Hamlyn Publishing Group Ltd, for the Hindu birthday poem from *Happy Birthdays Round the World*, by Lois Johnson.
The Reverend Peter Harrison, vicar of Beverley Minster, for the reference to the Soldiers' Chapel used in the story of *The Mouse Man*.
Rupert Hart Davis and Granada Publishing for a short extract from *The Morning Cockerel Book of Readings* by Margaret E. Rose.
Help the Aged for information about the care of the elderly.
Hodder and Stoughton for an extract from *The Ascent of Everest* by John Hunt.
John Murray (Publishers) Ltd, for the quotation of eight lines of a poem by Ronald Ross.
The Oxford University Press and the author for a reference to *The Latchkey Children* by Eric Allen.
The Oxford and Cambridge University Presses for quotations from the New English Bible, second edition © 1970, by permission.
The Directors of the Robert Thompson Craftsmen for factual information used in building up the story of *The Mouse Man*.
The Royal National Lifeboat Institution for a report in *The Lifeboat*, April 1971, used as the basis of the story, *The Picnic Which Lasted All Night*.

If any rights have been inadvertently overlooked, apologies are made and acknowledgement will be given in future editions if the author or publishers are informed.

Introduction

IN RECENT YEARS rapid changes have taken place in the provision of religious education in our Primary schools, changes brought about by a growing awareness of the ways in which children learn, of the capacity for religious thinking in children, and of the needs of children from a wide variety of racial, cultural and religious backgrounds. In spite of the revolution in religious education and the rapid secularisation of our society, the law of the land so far remains unchanged and opportunities for religious education and school Assembly are still offered in terms of the provisions laid down in the 1944 Education Act.

This is not to say that the curriculum and practice of the schools remain unchanged. Religious education in schools is being modified in response to the recognised needs of children. New syllabuses and books of suggestions from local education authorities, as well as more recently the work of the Schools Council project on Primary religious education (Working Paper 44), have also given an impetus to a re-analysis of the provisions of religious education in the classroom. It is the practice of the schools, as it develops in the next few years, which will affect future provisions of the law with respect to religious education. Meanwhile, experiment is encouraged on all sides.

The frequently quoted Plowden report, *Children and their Primary Schools*, spoke of the value of the school Assembly and made suggestions for the modification of the law. A large number of schools prefer to hold Assembly at some time other than the beginning of the day and increasing opportunity is given to children and teachers to conduct it. This book, then, suggests ways in which more people, children and adults, visitors and teachers, can be involved in providing ideas or experiences through which the school community may express a sense of wonder, give thanks, indicate concern for others and come to some understanding, at a practical level, of the religious activities which are practised in the homes of children in the school.

One of the new factors in our new society is the increasing interest in

8

the mystical religions of the East, another is the growing readiness for inter-faith discussions and activities. Now, as never before, children are asking questions about the religious practices of other children in the school, for they notice the absence of Jewish children on the Day of Atonement or, at dinner time, they hear a Muslim child refuse the meat pie because it contains ham. If understanding is to grow, opportunity must be made in class and in school gatherings for children to share their special feast days, and to tell the stories which have significance in their family religious practices. Some of the Assemblies in this book suggest how such sharing may be accomplished.

In recent years, through the study of Rudolf Laban's movement principles, we have come to realise the possibilities of helping children to explore ideas through movement, dance and mime. At the same time there has been a revolution in the approach to music-making in the schools, thanks to the pioneer work of Carl Orff. Through these media, children have a chance to explore ideas which are just beginning to stimulate their minds at a stage when they are not yet ready to verbalise such ideas at an abstract level of reasoning.

Since we are looking for ways in which children can contribute together in explorations in Assembly, here are two means of involvement which deserve wider use. As children grow in familiarity with the language of movement they may contribute more readily to Assembly themes by sharing, for example, the explorations begun in a physical education session. Thus, what began as a means of expressing an idea for the group themselves becomes something to communicate to others in visual terms. Similarly, castanets and tambourines, as well as recorders and chime bars, may be used to convey the ideas children have built up in music groups. At first, the theme will need some explanation, as suggested in the following text, for children who have not participated in the 'thinking and moving' or music-making class work. In schools where such methods are encouraged we may expect a growing spontaneity in the children's response.

This book does not attempt to provide material for the whole year. The writer has taken a number of themes which occur frequently in class work, in order to suggest varied ways in which children can contribute to the Assembly.

The amount of material is often greater than the head teacher would wish to include in any one Assembly and it is not suggested that these patterns should be the only ones used. To involve children in Assembly planning and conduct means a lot of extra work for both children and teachers if a high standard is to be maintained and if the ideas are to be worked out by the boys and girls. It is hoped that these suggestions might be used alongside other Assembly patterns so that variety is as wide as possible.

In this period of change, many attempts are being made to fill gaps in the provision of contemporary material. The head teacher will be on the alert for the publication of new sources and anxious to determine their value. This book points to materials in print at the time of writing; obviously, equally or more suitable material may be found in more recent collections.

There is a shortage of information describing in the detail Juniors demand, the many religious festivals practised on the Indian sub-continent and now undergoing some modification amongst the immigrant population in this country. One or two general examples of the most widely practised festivals are given in these pages, but in areas where there is a large Sikh, Hindu or Muslim population, it is suggested that teachers get all the relevant information they can from local leaders.

The mixture of material is deliberate! *When I needed a neighbour* may be sung one day and *All creatures of our God and king* the next; one day thought may be given to the Holi festival celebrated by some Hindu children in the school; on the next, a saint's day from the Christian calendar may be given attention. It is the experiences of the children in our particular school and neighbourhood which determine the subjects and materials we introduce. However, it will be seen that the book draws most heavily on Christian sources, using prayers and hymns which have established themselves through long usage as well as newer material which attempts to express the changes in theological emphasis and to cater for the new approaches in religious education which characterise the present day.

The use of traditional material does not suggest a rigid formality in the Assembly. There will be occasions when the head teacher may wish to suggest that the children close their eyes for a time of reflection; there will be other occasions when the most truly prayerful attitude will be to look together at some beautiful thing brought into the hall. There will be occasions when the children will group informally round a guitarist; there may be times when it is necessary to sit in a more organised way because of the position of a projector. In other words, worship must not be thought of as a particular type of action or a particular form of words.

For adults brought up in a Christian tradition attitudes and materials that belong to worship represent the accumulated tradition of centuries and this is what gives them their meaning. The same may be said of adults practising other world religions, deeply committed to their sacred writings and long established practices. Adults need to recollect in planning Assembly that children do not have such feelings of heritage and commitment, or only grasp their importance as they sense their significance to the adults they respect and love.

These Assemblies, then, try to suggest opportunities through which children can share delight and make a response, although not necessarily through the materials commonly associated with the word 'worship'. In a number of instances the songs written by the children themselves (e.g. one expressing their concern about forms of prejudice they recognise) and their poems (e.g. a boy's expression of wonder at the emergence of a butterfly from its chrysalis) will have more meaning than those derived from the writer's repertoire. It may be that explorations of this sort will lead children into true moments of worship and may justify the confidence placed in the Assembly by some of those associated with the formulation of the Plowden report.

A Wonderful World

'Coo! Look!' may be the reaction of a boy watching a butterfly's emergence from its chrysalis. His observation may be crudely expressed; he may try to hide his delight from his friends, but it is through such discoveries about the magic and rhythm of the world of nature that children may be helped to express their wonder. Some children will want to share their delight, building up displays for the school hall, which focus attention on the aspects which have given them pleasure. Some may wish to choose poems or prose which please them. In rare cases, the wonder may be related by the child to the gifts of God the Creator; more often children may find it sufficient simply to acknowledge their sense of joy at the natural world.

Sun, moon and stars

Present material suggesting how people in every age have told stories or written poems about these wonders. For example, the group whose work centres on the stars might recall and dramatise the Greek legend of the bears.

Juno, queen of the gods, was jealous of Callisto's beauty. Meeting the girl in the forest, Juno gazed intently at her. Embarrassed, Callisto looked down and was horrified to see that her feet had changed into hairy paws. Hurrying to the nearest pool mirror, she saw that she had been turned into a bear by the jealous queen.

Years later, Callisto's son, Arcas, saw a bear moving towards him and naturally did not recognise his mother. He raised his spear to kill the animal but Jupiter intervened. To save the life of Callisto, he turned Arcas into a bear, too, and to keep them safe from Juno's anger he put them up into the sky.

Read part of Ecclus. 43: 1–10 or Gen. 1: 1–4, 14–18 and sing *We thank you, Lord of heaven.*

Snow and frost
On a black background display patterns to suggest the symmetry and variety of snowflakes; link with the story of the photographer, Wilson Bentley, who took hundreds of pictures of snow crystals, and poems, e.g. Ecclus. 43: 13–20, Walter de la Mare, *Snow* or *The Snowflake*, Melville Cane, *Snow Toward Evening*. Alternatively, a film might introduce the theme, *Animals in Winter* or *Children in Winter*.

Tell the story of Bernard and the dog which found a missing traveller in the snow, the story of Martin of Tours arriving in Amiens one snowy day and cutting his cloak in two to share with a shivering beggar, or a child's story of a helicopter food lift to a snowbound village. A prayer might be written along these lines:

> We give thanks for the wonders of winter
> > for the sparkle of the snow
> > for the delicate patterns of frost
> > for the quietness of falling snow
> > for the noisy fun of snowballing.
> We remember
> > those who are afraid of avalanches
> > the old who suffer from the cold
> > and those stranded in snow drifts.

The seasons of the year

One way of sharing delight in the changing seasons of the year is through looking at colour transparencies, linked with a commentary prepared by the children. If the teacher does not have a personal collection of suitable slides from which the class can make a selection, use frames cut from a filmstrip, e.g., *The Seasons*. The following outline includes scripted material prepared by Junior children for their slide choice. Such lines could be spoken by the children themselves.

Slide 1: Red berries, rowan and rose hip,

Slide 2: Ripe corn, yellow and tall,

Slide 3: Falling leaves, orange and brown,

Slide 4: We give thanks for the colours of autumn.

Slide 5: The crisp snow, so white and unmarked in the morning,

Slide 6: The crazy pattern made by frost on the window pane,

Slide 7: We enjoy the fun of throwing snowballs.

Song: *When puddles freeze in the glittering lane.*

Slide 8: For now the winter is past . . . the flowers appear in the countryside,

Slide 9: The time is coming when the birds will sing (Song of Sol. 2: 11, 12, NEB).

Slide 10: We give thanks for the newness of spring.

Slide 11: Bright sun, long shadows,

Slide 12: Crinkled shells and slippery seaweed,

Slide 13: Tall blue delphiniums,

Slide 14: Small white daisies,

Slide 15: We enjoy summer days in the open air.

Song: *All things bright and beautiful* or *For the beauty of the earth,* vv. 1, 2.

Narrator: We give thanks for those who help us to enjoy the seasons
the photographer whose pictures remind us of the beauty of
the autumn
the miner digging coal to keep us warm in winter
the gardener who plants tulips in the park
the coach driver who takes us to the seaside in summer.

Story: Tell the story of Carl Linnaeus, or make up a story based on the
work of W. Keble Martin.

Whenever he had free time, the Rev. W. Keble Martin went into the
country in search of wild flowers. Sometimes he made his drawings of
them on the train when he was on the way home; by the time he was
eighty he had a collection of 1,400 drawings. His beautiful drawings have
been made into a book, *The Concise British Flora in Colour,* and several were
used for a set of postage stamps.

Prayer: (to be said together)
May we go round the world with open eyes to see its beauty.
May we go round the world with open ears to hear its lovely
sounds.
May we go round the world with open hands to share its
loveliness with other people.

Record: *What a wonderful world,* Louis Armstrong.

My Neighbour

MANY JUNIORS have a growing sense of concern which finds practical expression in collecting newspapers for the local Scouts' Association or in saving ice-cream money for the Save the Children Fund. The head teacher may wish to stimulate an examination of the contemporary significance of the lawyer's question (Luke 10: 29) through its presentation in Assembly. In the early part of the week he could pose the question and suggest one way in which needs are being met, whilst children carry out research to present at the final Assembly of the week. Such a theme might be taken in May, associated with Christian Aid week, or in June, when World Children's Day is recognised.

More subtle is the question of neighbourliness as it affects the children's own relationships. Most head teachers will feel that this aspect is best tackled in smaller groups, as children work on the theme in the classroom.

Who is my neighbour?

Tell a story based on Luke 10: 25–29 to set the scene for the week's thinking.

> There was quite a crowd jostling round the man who was speaking. Some looked strong and healthy. Some of those pressing forward seemed thin and sick. Several men stood at the edge of the eager crowd, grouped together as if they did not want to get too close to the poorer folk.
>
> It was a man in this group who spoke to Jesus. 'Sir', he said, 'I have a question to ask you. What must I do to be sure of eternal life?' Jesus looked at him; he knew that these men studied the law. 'What does the law say?' he replied. 'Love the Lord your God with all your heart, with all your strength and with all your mind.' Jesus waited, and then the man continued. 'It goes on, Love your neighbour as yourself.' 'That's right,' said Jesus. 'That is the answer to your question. Love God and your neighbour. Do those two things and you will live.' Then the man put his second question. 'But, sir, answer me this one, Who is my neighbour?'

Read Luke 10: 30–35 in a modern translation, first reminding the children of the antagonism between Jews and Samaritans.

Introduce *When I needed a neighbour* as a song through which Sydney Carter has tried to arouse concern for others.

A home for my neighbour

A picture of the Good Samaritan story would be a reminder of the week's theme. The Paula Jordan picture is particularly striking for older children; a more colourful but smaller illustration is given in *The Miracles and Parables of Jesus*. Play a record of or sing *When I needed a neighbour*.

Talk about conditions which led reformers to start homes for children and tell story of Pestalozzi, Thomas Stephenson or Dr. Barnardo. In circumstances where it is unwise to concentrate on children's homes, use the story of Leonard Cheshire's vain search on behalf of a gravely ill friend, which led to his establishment of homes for the disabled and chronically sick.

Sing *We must help the poor and needy*; a prayer might follow these lines:

> We thank you, God our Father, for our homes
> for the love of parents, brothers and sisters
> for good food and comfortable beds.
> We pray, God our Father, for those who have no homes
> for refugees made homeless in time of war
> for children without parents.
> We remember, God our Father, those who act as neighbours to
> the homeless
> the staff of the Cheshire Homes
> those who write advertisements for Shelter.
> Help us to be good neighbours.

Good neighbours

Song: *When I needed a neighbour,* v. 1.

Narrator: On Monday a boy left the newspaper on the mat. It stayed there all day, but no one noticed. On Tuesday he left another paper beside the first one. They stayed there all day, but no one noticed. On Wednesday the milkman asked, 'Has anyone seen Mrs. Jones?' The police found that Mrs. Jones had fallen and hurt herself. For two days her neighbours had been too busy to notice that something was wrong.

But it is not always like that. All through the ages people have tried to be good neighbours.

Teacher 1: Listen to this report: 'Hilda is elderly. She existed in two damp rooms in North London. No electricity. No proper toilet. The only source of water was a cold tap in the back yard. . . .' Through their advertisement *Help the Aged* lets everyone know of the need of elderly people. Are there any good neighbours who can help?

Child 1: Our local Council has opened a centre where old people can meet together for tea.

Child 2: Mr. Snips the barber charges less money when he cuts the hair of old age pensioners.

Child 3: Children at Sittingbourne joined in a sponsored swim for *Help the Aged* and raised £350 to house two old people in new flats.

Song: *When they needed a neighbour, help was there.*

Teacher 2: The National Health Service makes medical treatment available for everyone, but there are neighbourly people who give extra help to the sick and disabled.

Child 4:   Mr. Brown has joined the Hospital Car Service; he uses his car to take people for hospital treatment or visiting.

Child 5:   The Corporation of Hull has opened Isaac Robinson House where young disabled people can stay.

Teacher 2:   Our history books tell stories of good neighbours long ago. 'Your majesty, please grant me a piece of land.' King Henry I looked in amazement at his jester. 'But what do you want with land?' he asked. 'Sire, I want to build a hospital for the people of London.' So Rahere was given a plot of land at Smithfield and today you can see the hospital of St. Bartholomew; in the church nearby is the tomb of Rahere the jester who wanted to be a good neighbour to the sick.

Song: *When they needed a neighbour, help was there.*

Narrator: The holy book of the Muslims says:

Feed the hungry, visit the sick. Show kindness to orphans, to your neighbours and to the traveller on the road.

The law of the Jews says:

You shall love your neighbour as a man like yourself (Lev. 19: 18, NEB).

Jesus finished his story of the good Samaritan with a question to the lawyer. 'Tell me,' he said, 'who was the good neighbour to the injured man?' The lawyer was forced to say, 'The man who showed him kindness.' 'Go and do the same,' replied Jesus.

Song: *When I needed a neighbour.*

Glad Days

THE TRANSITION from the Infants' to the Junior school can be a difficult one and some children find the apparent impersonality of the larger department uncomfortable or frightening. This is particularly true at times of communal activities like meals and Assembly. Near the beginning of the school year it would be wise to have some Assembly themes which contain familiar elements. The birthday recognition commonly celebrated in the Infants' school might be one such topic, linking it, for the sake of the older children who could despise such 'infant' pleasures, with celebrations of other types and those from other parts of the world. This second element would provide an opportunity to share the experiences of children who have lived in other countries. The birthday celebration could be the first of the sequence, going on to other seasonal glad days, such as half term holiday, hallowe'en or a saint's day.

A holiday

Play a record of music which suggests a holiday mood. One choice could be *The Little Train of the Caipira*, from *Bachianas Brasileiras*, first telling how Heitor Villa-Lobos wrote the music in an hour when he was having a bumpy ride on a little narrow gauge railway.

Talk about a coming class expedition, things which children might do during the half term holiday or listen to stories or poems of children's real or imaginary adventures during a school holiday.

If there are children familiar with holiday festivities in other countries, let them share information about such events, preferably in a dramatised scene, by dressing up or with songs. For example, children from Bengal might tell about the October festival of Durga, the patron goddess of that State.

According to the legend, Durga killed the demon of evil, which had hidden inside a water buffalo. At the festival a statue of the goddess, made of sun-dried mud, and another of the demon with a buffalo's head are taken in procession, mounted on a decorated bullock cart and accompanied by drums and cymbals, to the river. Here they are thrown into the water with garlands of flowers.

A saint's day

October 4 is St. Francis' day and it would be appropriate to tell his story during this season, since this saint seems particularly popular with younger children. Suggest three aspects of his life, with the help of a filmstrip made by children, a mural or mimed incidents:

a. his care for animals and birds

Francis met a boy on his way to market with a cage of doves. Francis paid for the birds and set them free.

b. telling the story of Jesus

Francis wanted to make the Christmas story come alive for the villagers and it is said that the first Christmas crib scene was the one he arranged at Greccio, with real actors and animals.

c. sharing friendship

When Francis' eyes became weak, his friends were glad to look after him and as he composed his hymn of joy one of them wrote down the words, so that they might all join in.

Sing selected verses of *All creatures of our God and king*, based on his *Canticle of the Sun*, and use the prayer associated with Francis:

Lord, make me an instrument of thy peace.
  Where there is hatred, let me sow love
  Where there is injury, pardon
  Where there is doubt, faith
  Where there is despair, hope
  Where there is darkness, light
  Where there is sadness, joy.

Birthdays

Make a pinata and hang it in the hall, to be struck down by a group of children chosen by the younger child who has a birthday on this day. (A pinata is a papiermâché or clay animal shape containing small presents or sweets.)

Action: Light candles on a birthday ring.

Song: *Happy birthday to you.*

Leader: Today we share ——'s birthday and have a chance to think about the ways in which birthdays are celebrated in different parts of the world.

Slides: The Queen has an official birthday, usually on the second Saturday of June, as well as her own family birthday celebration. On this special day many people watch the celebrations at Horse Guards' Parade and listen to the cannons firing in honour of the Queen.

Reporter: A Hindu boy in India gets up early on his birthday and dresses in his best clothes. He stands in front of a picture of his Hindu gods and sings a song.

Song or reading: This is my birthday.
I am the creation of the Almighty.
Give me energy and wisdom
To serve my friends and parents.
I wish to do all my work

According to the will of God.
Help me not to cheat, not to speak untruths,
To honour the elderly, to serve others.
Guide me in proper ways
So that I may live
A long and happy life,
For this is my birthday.

From *Happy Birthdays Round the World.*

Leader: In Mexico there are surprises in the pinata which hangs from the ceiling for the birthday boy or girl.

Action: Chosen children break the pinata.

Story: A Mexican birthday story.

Grandfather painted a tiger pinata for Pedro's birthday and sold his precious guitar so that there was enough money to stuff the pinata with sweets and toys for the children's party.

Prayer: We give thanks for the people who share our birthdays
for those who give us presents
for the postman who brings our birthday cards.
We give thanks for the fun of birthdays
for the excitement of unwrapping parcels
for the party we have with our friends.
We give thanks for other special days when we remember the birthdays of great men and women who have served the peoples of the world.

Song: *Up my neighbour,* or a birthday song made up by the children.

People with Courage

SEVERAL NEWER syllabuses introduce themes which help children to examine qualities of life; the West Riding's *Suggestions for Religious Education* is one which invites enquiry into different aspects of courage. Juniors admire courage in the lives of others and the theme has proved popular as well as wide-ranging.

Few Juniors would admit to fear, but many children do have periods of acute anxiety and a concealed sense of fear, perhaps particularly at the top of the Primary school, when pressures build up over changes of school and physical development. At the beginning of this week, therefore, a negative aspect of the theme is used in the hopes that it may encourage more open conversation about the fears of the older children.

Overcoming fear
Read children's stories of adventures in which they have overcome their fears or tell the legend of Matafu. A full version is given in *The Boy Who Was Afraid*, but this would need to be serialised over several days. Here is the basic legend.

> The Polynesian boy was regarded as an outcaste by the rest of his tribe because he was frightened by the sea, the result of a canoe accident when he was small. Matafu was ashamed and set out to conquer his fear. Accompanied by his dog and his pet albatross, his adventures included killing a dangerous shark and a wild boar, as well as making a new canoe when his own was wrecked.

Some teachers may wish to suggest a time of reflection, drawing material from ideas put forward by the children,
> e.g. Let us think of times when we have been afraid.

Some of us are afraid of nightmares and of the dark.
May we have courage to overcome our fear.
Some of us are afraid to own up when we have done wrong.
May we have courage to overcome our fear.
Some of us are afraid of pain.
May we have courage at all times.
Some of us are afraid of being laughed at.
May we have courage at all times.

Courage to make a new life
Individual children might be prepared to show the difficulties involved in overcoming some physical limitation (e.g. to paint with a brush held in the mouth, or to play table tennis sitting in a chair) in order to appreciate the perseverance of those who have mastered such skills to give themselves an independent and full life. Continue with one of the following examples.

Show the picture of a boy painting with the brush held in his mouth (*Themes in Religious Education,* Set 2) and tell the story of Elizabeth Twistington Higgins, who paints pictures of ballet dancers now that polio has stopped her own dancing days.

Play music Beethoven wrote after he became deaf and which he never heard (e.g. *The Hymn of Joy* from his ninth symphony). Use part of the prayer Beethoven wrote when he realised that his deafness could not be cured,

i.e. O God, give me strength to be victorious over myself . . .

O guide my spirit and raise me from these dark depths . . .

For thou alone understandest and canst inspire me.

Tell the story of Lady Susan Masham; her sustained efforts on behalf of other disabled people led to the offer of a life peerage.

A festival of courage

If each class does research on aspects of courage, the children might prepare life-size paper mosaics of the particular hero to whom they wish to draw attention in the Assembly.

Group 1: We salute those who show courage in their daily work.

Mime: A scene depicting a dangerous moment in one occupation, e.g. firemen trying to rescue a child from a smoke-filled room.

Group 2: We salute those who show courage in emergencies.

Story flash 1: Fourteen-year-old Brian Gibbon was awarded the George Medal for saving his nephew, Tommy, when an aeroplane hit their home and set it on fire.

Group 3: We honour those who have had the courage to make new lives for themselves after crippling accidents.

Story flash 2: Danny Hearn played rugby until his neck was broken in a match against the New Zealand All Blacks. He has gone back to his job as a teacher—a man in a wheelchair, a man with courage.

Story flash 3: Mary Verghese was paralysed in an accident; it looked as if her career as a doctor was over. She operates from her wheelchair—mending the damaged hands of patients with leprosy.

Group 4: We honour those who have been prepared to die, rather than to give up the things they believe.

Record: Excerpt from *Roman Festivals*, with introduction. Trumpets greet the Emperor's arrival at the great arena, Circus Maximus. There is a moment of quiet as the Christians arrive, singing a hymn of joy. When the iron gates open, the roar of the lions is heard.

Story: Ignatius the martyr.

The soldiers marched briskly along the dusty road. Their prisoner stumbled against the chains that held him. 'Come along there,' the centurion ordered roughly and the soldiers jerked the old man along.

Ignatius, bishop of Antioch, was on his way to the Roman arena, arrested for his refusal to worship the Roman gods. Knowing that he would be thrown to the lions but unconcerned about himself, his mind was on others throughout the journey. 'My people in Antioch—how they must be suffering. I must do what I can to help them.'

At Smyrna his fellow Christians came out to greet him. 'Send helpers to my friends in Antioch,' he pleaded. 'Help them all you can.' 'But what do you need?' they cried. 'Nothing but some writing materials.' The guard gave him permission to write several letters. 'I am coming to Rome as a prisoner in chains,' he wrote in one letter. 'I go to my death willingly for the sake of Jesus.'

In Rome the great arena was packed; huge crowds had come to see the excitement. 'Look at the Christian,' they cried as the old man was brought into the arena. Then the iron door opened. 'Listen to the lions,' they cried. Perhaps only the Roman Christians remembered what brave Ignatius had written, 'I go to my death willingly for the sake of Jesus.'

Song: *I sing a song of the saints of God.*

Prayer: Give us courage
                          to speak the truth
                          to be loyal to our friends
                          to be fearless in times of danger
                          to be brave when we are hurt
                          to help other people.

Festivals of Light

DURING THE early winter months several of the world's religious groups hold festivals in which lights play an important part. In a multi-racial school there should be opportunities for children from different religious backgrounds to share their delight in their festivals and to see the similarity of the symbolism representing the triumph of light over darkness.

For information about the actual dates of the celebrations teachers may consult religious leaders or *World Religions: Aids for Teachers*.

The feast of Divali

Decorate the hall with lights, clay saucer lamps made by children or night lights in small jars, to represent the veranda decorations in Indian homes in October/November at Divali time. Younger Asian children might be asked to display saris, Indian toys and musical instruments. One of the mothers or a teacher might tell the story traditionally associated with this time of the year.

Long ago, the story says, there was a king in India who was growing old. 'One of my sons must rule in my place,' he said and he chose Prince Rama, whom all the people loved because of his courage. But one of the king's wives, Kaikeyi, the mother of Prince Bharata, was angry that her son was not chosen. Craftily, she tricked the old king into making her a promise. 'I swear that I shall do whatever you wish,' he said. 'Banish Prince Rama for fourteen years,' she replied. The king could not break his promise and Rama went into the forest.

King Dasharamtha was heartbroken and soon died, so Prince Bharata, deeply upset by his mother's treachery, went in search of Rama. 'Our father is dead,' he said. 'Come back and reign over us.' Rama refused. 'I was banished for fourteen years,' he said. 'I will not return until that time is over.' 'Give me your golden sandals,' replied Bharata. 'I will put them on the throne which is your rightful place. I will not sit on the throne but I will govern the people until you return to claim your sandals and your throne.'

At last the fourteen years were over. Rama's brother went to fetch him. 'Let us all go to meet Rama,' cried the people, and they hurried out of their houses with little clay lamps in their hands to light their way through the dark forest. It was a day of great rejoicing when King Rama claimed his sandals and his throne, a day of light after a time of darkness.

The feast of Hanukkah
Borrow an eight-branched Hanukkah candlestick for the table. One of the Jewish children might light the first candle, saying one of the traditional prayers:

> Praised be Thou, O Lord our God, Ruler of the world,
>   who has granted us life and has sustained us to
>   celebrate this joyous festival.

Tell or read a story based on 1 Maccabees 4: 36–59 and the legend associated with the candlestick; when the priests came to relight their seven-branched Temple candlestick they found only a small amount of oil but, miraculously, it lasted eight days until more oil could be prepared.

In a small school Jewish children may describe their home celebrations at Hanukkah, their games and the giving of presents. Where this is not practical, read an extract from the diary of Anne Frank, the Jewish girl hiding in an Amsterdam attic; the entry for December 7, 1942, describes their Hanukkah.

Sing *All people that on earth do dwell*, based on Psalm 100, reminding the children that these words have been used to remember God's goodness for hundreds of years.

The light of Christmas
The props needed for this service, introducing German and Czech customs, are an Advent wreath and the ingredients for the Christingles.

Narrator: It was dark and late in the day when Joseph and Mary arrived at the inn.

Child 1:   'No room! No room!' was the inn-keeper's cry.

Child 2:   'Please find us a corner,' said Joseph.

Child 3:	So the inn-keeper took them into the dark stable.
Narrator:	And the light shone, for in that dark stable Jesus was born.
Action:	Light the first candle on the wreath.
Song:	*The world was in darkness* or *Mary set out on a winter's night.*
Narrator:	It was dark on the hillside where the shepherds were guarding their sheep.
Child 1:	'I don't like the dark,' said one shepherd.
Child 2:	A light began to gleam in the sky.
Child 3:	Then the shepherd who didn't like the dark was afraid of the light, until he knew what it meant.
Narrator:	And the light shone, for the shepherd knew that Jesus was born.
Action:	Light the second candle.
Song:	*The first nowell,* vv. 1, 2.
Narrator:	It was dark in the desert.
Child 1:	'Follow the star,' said one wise man.
Child 2:	'See its light,' said a second.
Child 3:	So they went on their way through city and village.
Narrator:	And the light shone over the place where the young child lay.
Action:	Light the third candle.
Song:	*The first nowell,* vv. 3–5.
Narrator:	The light began to shine for an old man.

Child 1:   Mary and Joseph brought Jesus to Jerusalem.

Child 2:   An old man, Simeon, saw the baby, took him in his arms and blessed him.

Child 3:   'Now light has come to the world,' said old Simeon.

Narrator: And the light shone out into the world.

Action: Light the fourth candle.

Narrator: (Link actions to the spoken word).
Take an orange.
Fix a candle on top of it.
Fasten wooden sticks of raisins and sweets in the orange.
Light the candle.
This Christingle candle is the present which children in Czechoslovakia used to carry out into the street at Christmas time. What did it mean?
The orange reminded them of the world in which they lived.
The candle helped them to remember the light of Jesus coming to the world.
The sweets reminded them of the good things Jesus brought.
And as the Czech children carried the lighted Christingle into the street they remembered the light of Jesus' love going into the dark places of the world.

Child 1:   The light goes to places where people are homeless. (He lights a Christingle candle.)

Child 2:   The light goes to places where people are hungry. (She lights a Christingle.)

Prayer: We give thanks for the way in which light shines in dark places
for the light which comes to the hungry
for the light which comes to the homeless
for the light which comes to the lonely
when other people follow the way that Jesus taught.

Song: *Silent night* or *We wish you a merry Christmas.*

31

People and Places

IN SPITE OF the wider world introduced to children by television, their life is naturally bound by the confines of their own experience in town or village. Juniors accept the pattern of the life they know and perhaps school Assembly can provide a chance for them to look with gratitude at those things which are close at hand. Following these themes in whatever order seems most appropriate might help children to understand that, whether one lives in city or country, there are common pleasures for which to give thanks and similar responsibilities to be shared.

In the country
Use a record, *Sounds of the Countryside* or *Songs of British Birds*, and a picture display of country scenes as a lead-in. Tell how John Clare delighted in the discoveries he made in the Northamptonshire countryside. He was not a good speller; he often forgot commas and full-stops; but he used his talents to record the beauty he saw. Read a poem appropriate to the season. For example:

The Thrush's Nest

Within a thick and spreading hawthorn bush,
    That overhung a molehill large and round,
I heard from morn to morn a merry thrush
    Sing hymns to sunrise, and I drank the sound
With joy; and, often an intruding guest,
    I watched her secret toils from day to day—
How true she warped the moss to form a nest,
    And modelled it within with wood and clay;
And by and by, like heath-bells gilt with dew,

There lay her shining eggs, as bright as flowers,
Ink-spotted-over shells of greeny blue;
And there I witnessed in the sunny hours
A brood of nature's minstrels chirp and fly,
Glad as that sunshine and the laughing sky.

John Clare.

Sing *To God who makes all lovely things* or *All things which live below the sky.*

Invite an adult who loves the country to talk briefly about some aspect of country life, such as finding a badger's sett. Alternatively, a group of children might act a scene showing disregard for country things, like a boy who leaves a gate open and is dismayed to find that his dog chases sheep out on to the road.

Down to the sea

A display of seashore 'finds' or a filmstrip, *Life on the Seashore,* will help the children to appreciate the beauty of rock pools and cliffs.

Play a sea shanty or ask a class to sing one, to recall the work of sailors past and present, bringing goods to our docks, carrying passengers or going out with the fishing fleet. Sing *When lamps are lighted in the town* and use a prayer of concern:

O God, we remember those whose work takes them out to sea
    sailors in ocean liners
    fishermen on the trawlers
    pilots who guide boats into harbour.
O God, we remember those who stay at home while their
                    menfolk are at sea
    the wives of men in the herring fleet
    children whose fathers are away for long months.
O God, we remember those whose work is dangerous
    men in the engine room
    men on oil tankers
Protect and guide all those who sail the seven seas.

Read Psalm 107: 23–30 or tell a story of bravery in sea rescue, e.g., Grace Darling, Paul in the storm (Acts 27: 1–20, 27–28: 2) or a contemporary example. Sing the first verse of *Eternal Father, strong to save,* recalling that it was written by William Whiting when a pupil at the Winchester Choristers' School was about to sail for America.

Our town

As the children come into the hall play a record, *Street Noises* or *The Cockaigne Overture.*

Narrator: We hurry to school, still half asleep, and we miss the sounds and sights which could give us pleasure. We hurry home on a winter's day and we take for granted the street lamps which light our way. Let us give thanks for the joys of our town.

Hymn: Come, let us remember the joys of the town:
Gay vans and bright buses that roar up and down,
Shop windows and playgrounds and swings in the park,
And street lamps that twinkle in rows after dark.

And let us remember the life in the street:
The horses that pass us, the dogs that we meet,
Grey pigeons, brown sparrows and gulls from the sea,
And folk that are friendly to you and to me.

Come let us now lift up our voices in praise,
And to the Creator a thanksgiving raise,
For towns with their buildings of stone, steel and wood,
For people who love them and work for their good.
by permission of Doris Gill.

Narrator: We meet many people along the street on our way to school, the postman tramping down the road in all weathers, the sweeper who cleans up the pavement, the policeman ready to help the traveller who has lost his way.

Poem: *We Thank You,* L. E. Cox.

Narrator: Along the street or behind its closed doors there may be people in our town who need help.

Dramatisation: Groups of children act out prepared scenes, e.g., a small child is lost in a crowded shop and a supervisor takes him to the enquiry desk; a blind lady is helped across the road.

Narrator: When we stop to think about the help given in our town, we remember those living here long ago who found ways of helping, a man who put up a drinking trough for the horses which pulled heavy carts, the Council which opened a play area for children, a lady whose money built homes for old people.

Prayer: For lovely things in towns and cities
    for petrol rainbows in puddles
    for plane trees and window boxes
        We give thanks.
    For the people who work in our town
    for the women in the biscuit factory
    for the ice-cream man and the grocer
        We give thanks.
    For the people who help others in our town
    the nurses at the clinic
    for the librarian who arranges story time
        We give thanks.

Hymn: *The lights go up all over the town* or *Lights go up at night in the city.*

A Story to Tell

IN A WEEK when one of the classes has prepared a puppet play for sharing with the school or the children are going to look round a local theatre, it may be appropriate to take an Assembly theme which suggests how a much loved story has been interpreted and shared through the arts. In many schools it would be appropriate to use the story of Jesus, providing material which can be followed up in the classroom.

Let's do a play

Play a record of an excerpt from a contemporary musical linked with the life of Jesus, e.g., *Godspell, Jesus Christ Superstar*, suggesting to the children that the story of Jesus has been told in many ways.

Give a word picture of the scene in a medieval market place as the crowds gathered round to watch the guilds perform their traditional plays. The story of Mak, inserted in the Wakefield cycle, suggests that humorous incidents were added to the biblical sequence to hold the attention of the crowd.

> The shepherds were asleep when Mak crept in and stole a lamb from the flock. He dashed home with it and his wife suggested that the lamb should be hidden in the empty cradle. When the shepherds came to search for their lamb, Mak told them that his wife had just had a baby, hoping this would make them go away. Instead, they looked in the cradle and teased Mak on the likeness of the child to his father. 'What a pity it has such a long nose!' In the end the thief was forced to return the stolen lamb and the shepherds tossed him in the blanket which had been wrapped round the animal in the cradle. Then the shepherds went on their way to Bethlehem to offer their gifts to Mary.

Read extracts from the New Testament narratives about the birth of Jesus, Matt. 2, Luke 2. Choose a hymn which continues the theme of the story of Jesus, such as *Jesus, good above all other.*

Writing the story down

Sing verses from a hymn which describes events in the life of Jesus (e.g. *Tell me the stories of Jesus, Gentle Christ*) and lead into a story of the gospel writer, Luke, based on the hypothesis that he used material he had collected himself, together with material from the so-called Q scroll and Mark. The narrative might begin in this way:

> The crowd gathered round the stranger, each one of them eager to tell him all he knew. First the old man spoke. 'The Master told the story so well,' he said. 'There was a shepherd who had one hundred sheep. . .' Doctor Luke reached for his notes. 'Let me get the story written down,' he begged.
>
> Then one of the younger men spoke. 'What I liked about Jesus was his care for the people who were ill. Do you remember the story we heard of the day Jesus helped ten lepers?' The others nodded. 'Let me write it down,' said Doctor Luke again.
>
> At the end Luke's fingers were stiff and his eyes tired. 'I am grateful for all your help. I want everyone to know the story of Jesus and I feel it ought to be written down now, whilst there are so many who remember the stories he told and the things he did. One day I will put the stories together for all to read.'

Read one or more familiar stories told only by this writer, e.g., Luke 2: 41–52; 15: 11–24; 19: 1–10.

The prayer might be an act of thanksgiving built up with suggestions made by the children, with their response, *We give thanks*, e.g.:

For stories of Jesus teaching the people. . . .
For stories of Jesus helping the lonely. . . .
For stories of Jesus healing the sick. . . .
For stories Jesus told which help us to learn the way of caring. . . .
For those who wrote down the stories of Jesus. . . .

Sharing the story across the world

Divide the Assembly theme into sections, so that several teachers can contribute to it. Each might tell how one aspect of the story of Jesus has been told, with the help of different art forms. A general outline is given; encourage the presentation of individual ideas!

Music:　　Excerpt from *Godspell* or *Jesus Christ Superstar*.

Narrator 1:　Poets and hymn-writers have helped to tell the story of Jesus so that it can be heard all over the world. One story says that the Austrian priest, Joseph Mohr, composed the words of *Silent night* one snowy, starlit night, as he walked home after a visit to a mother and her new baby. This carol has been translated into dozens of languages, and so the story of Jesus is shared across the world.

Reading:　　Luke 2: 4–7.

Song:　　*Silent night.*

Narrator 2:　Artists have helped to tell the story of Jesus.

Pictures:　　Show pictures in contrasting styles, e.g. the Nelson series prepared by nuns at a Cockfosters convent, others by world-famous artists, and those which suggest how Jesus is portrayed by artists of different races, such as *Christ in Art*, from *Themes in Religious Education*, set 2.

Narrator 2:　When we look at such pictures we remember the friends Jesus made and the ways in which he helped them.

Song:　　*At work beside his father's bench* or *Martha and Mary.*

Narrator 3: Music has helped to tell the story of Jesus, both in the theatre and in the church.

Record: Excerpt from *Procession of Palms.*

Reading: *The Donkey's Owner,* Clive Sansom.

Narrator 4: 'Teach us to pray,' the disciples said to Jesus. There is one prayer which is used all round the world by people who have heard the story of Jesus. This West Indian version is one of our favourite ways of joining together in the prayer Jesus taught.

Song: *Our Father, who art in heaven.*

Isn't He Clever!

'Isn't he clever!' exclaimed the child watching an artist sketching a tourist outside the National Portrait Gallery. Most Juniors have an admiration for some adult who seems to them to be particularly clever or skilled; it may be the drummer in the pop group of the moment or an artist whose work had been introduced on children's television. Often the admiration is sufficiently strong to encourage a child to tackle some task in order to become like the chosen hero.

Some teachers will feel that there is value in drawing attention to the lives of those who have recognised their personal talents as God-given, to be exploited to the full in a spirit of stewardship.

The gift of the musician

Let children choose a favourite record and introduce the music by saying something about the composer or performer,

> e.g. 'Have you thought of taking up singing?' his teacher asked Cliff Richard after he had played Ratty in a school production of *The Wind in the Willows*. Neither of them could have guessed that one day he would be 'Top of the Pops';
> Handel's father did not want to encourage his son's interest in music, but George Frederick practised the clavichord secretly at night. At last his father agreed that the boy's gift should not be neglected.

Alternatively, children may play tunes they have composed or sing songs they enjoy.

Some teachers may like to introduce *The Little Drummer Boy*, reminding the children of the legend of the boy who wanted to bring a gift to the baby Jesus, playing his drum for the child. Others may prefer the story of David using his musical skill to calm the sick King Saul (1 Sam. 16: 14–23), or the story of King David asking Asaph to compose music for the pro-

40

cession of the Ark of the Covenant entering Jerusalem (1 Chron. 15: 16–22; 16: 1–10).

Sing a hymn based on an ancient Hebrew song (e.g. *The Lord's my Shepherd, All people tha ton earth do dwell*).

The gift of the storyteller

Ask two or three teachers to tell or read short stories written or retold by great storytellers (e.g. Joan Aiken, Roger Lancelyn Green).

If preferred, take Bible illustrations (e.g. Jesus telling the story of the lost sheep to help people to understand the quality of God's love, Luke 15: 1–6) or read one of David Kossoff's Old Testament stories. Near Christmas the leader of Assembly might read Eleanor Farjeon's poem, *The Mother's Tale*, and lead into the gospel story of the nativity.

A third possibility is for a class to dramatise the story of Hans Christian Andersen as a schoolboy. The other pupils laughed at him, finding him rather odd, and he got into trouble for daydreaming until someone discovered his gift for words and encouraged him to write and tell stories. Read an extract from one of his stories (e.g. *The Ugly Duckling*).

Sing verses made up by the children as their expression of thanksgiving for books and storytellers. The following is one example, using the tune set to *Thank you for ev'ry new good morning*:

Thank you for books of great adventure
Thank you for stories old and new
Thank you for all the story tellers
who make dreams come true.

The gift of craftsmanship

Set up tables showing crafts carried out by different classes or arrange pictures of craftsmen, whose type of work is known in the district (e.g. thatcher, glass-blower, well-dresser). One group of children might prepare a sequence of pictures illustrating the suggested reading from the Apocrypha.

During Assembly tell a story linked with the theme, one which is internationally known (e.g. Michelangelo's sculpture of David, cut from a partly-worked piece of marble abandoned by another sculptor years before), or one of local significance, like the example given below.

Introduction: One man does his work in a hurry and we call him a poor workman. Another man does his work carefully and we call him a craftsman.

Child 1: In our homes we live with the work of craftsmen,

Child 2: the men who designed chairs and beds,

Child 3: the weaver who made cushion material,

Child 4: the plumber who fixed the pipes for our water supply.

Child 1: When we go out to play we find which of our toys have been carefully made,

Child 2: the cricket bat made of strong wood,

Child 3: the little car whose wheels go round,

Child 4: the doll that doesn't break, even though lots of children nurse her.

Reading: A writer of long ago spoke about the craftsmen of his day, Ecclus. 38: 27–31.

Song: *Like a great river flow the people.*

Story: Robert Thompson, the mouse man.

42

'See how many mice you can find,' said the Minster guide. The children stared and then giggled. 'It's not a joke,' Mr. Atkinson went on. 'In this soldiers' chapel there are several mice. See how many you can find and then I'll tell you about them.'

The children began exploring. Then Robert beckoned to the others. 'Come here,' he hissed. 'I've found a mouse carved on the side of this chair.' A moment later Margaret whispered, 'Here's another; it's running along the bottom of this chest.'

'Now, let me tell you about the mouse man,' said Mr. Atkinson. 'Robert Thompson learnt how to mend wooden gates, but he really wanted to use his skill to make beautiful things, like the oak carvings he had seen in Ripon Cathedral. "I shall use good English wood," said Robert Thompson, "so that we can make fine solid furniture which will last for years."

'But where does the mouse come into the story?' asked Margaret. 'The mouse began as a sort of joke,' said Mr. Atkinson. 'A carpenter didn't get particularly well paid for his good craftsmanship in the nineteenth century and it took long hours to do the careful work that Robert Thompson wanted. One day he was carving a beam for a church roof when one of his work-mates muttered, "Poor as church mice." Robert Thompson took up his small knife and carved a little mouse in the beam on which he was working.

'Afterwards he thought about the little mouse. "It chews at the wood, using its chisel-like teeth. Nobody takes much notice as it works carefully away. Why! that's rather like us," thought Mr. Thompson. "We work quietly and carefully at our carpentry and it does not matter if we are as poor as church mice. We are doing good work and that's worth a lot. The little mouse shall be *our* mouse. I'll put him on each piece of furniture we make, to show that it has been made carefully and well."

'So,' said Mr. Atkinson, 'the mouse is a sign of work well done by a master craftsman. And although Robert Thompson died in 1955, his work continues as the men in his workshop go on making fine furniture for churches and homes, each piece with its little carved mouse.'

Prayer: Good work, Bad work
Work done with care, Work done in a hurry
May we work well when we wash the plates
         when we do creative writing
         when we paint pictures
         and when we do mathematics.

Living with Danger

Most week's television news includes the story of someone's heroism. Children respond to such stories and an Assembly theme might consider the life of those whose daily task is concerned with danger and life-saving. Visiting firemen and policemen are hardly likely to talk about the dangers of their jobs, being more concerned to suggest ways in which children can act responsibly in the street and in using flammable materials. These school visitors might get a better reception if thought has been given, through indirect means, to the dangers they face because of accident or irresponsibility. If historical illustrations are used, as suggested in the following text, they should be chosen because of their connection with current school projects.

Fire! Fire!

A group might sing the round, *London's burning*; read a newspaper cutting about a fire or list children's suggestions about the causes of fire in home and factory.

Accounts which suggest the prompt action of people might be a suitable development. The Great Fire of London would be one possible illustration.

> Anxious to save the ancient buildings of the Inner Temple, the Duke of York did not waste time arguing with the lawyer who tried to delay his men when they brought up gunpowder to demolish the Paper House nearby. Even so, sparks caught the roof, but a sailor, Richard Rowe, clambered up the building and beat out the flames.

Another possible aspect would be a story of an Australian bush fire.

Thought should be given, too, to the bravery of people in times of fire. Share further extracts from current newspapers or children's creative writing about rescue attempts.

It may be appropriate to have a 'thinking about' time on these lines:

Think of the firemen who go into danger to save the lives of
people trapped by fire;
Think of the firemen who go into danger when factories are
ablaze;
Think of those who have been hurt in fires, especially those whose
bodies have been burnt.

We are grateful for the bravery of men in the fire service, for the
skill of the plastic surgeon, and for the care of doctors and
nurses.

Beneath the sea
As the children come into the hall play a record of sea sounds. Talk about
skin divers, the fascination of the under-water world they explore, the
treasures they find, both those of the natural world and those from old
wrecks. Read a poem, e.g. *The Diver*, by W. W. E. Ross, and talk about
ideas for a prayer expressing a sense of wonder at the under-water world.

e.g. Seaweeds waving to and fro
Shoals of darting fish
Pearls and sponges hiding in the deeps
For all the wonders of life in the sea
We give thanks, O God.
Barnacles encrusted on an ancient wreck
Hiding its long lost treasures
For the skill of divers working on the sea bed
We give thanks, O God.

Lead into the story of an occasion when frogmen were needed to save
life.

Most of the crew were trapped when the Danish dredger, *Captain
Neilson*, turned over in Moreton Bay, Australia, on 18th September, 1964.
One man swam to get help and frogmen went to the rescue, saving all the
crew.

45

S.O.S.

Build up a display of literature linked with the work of the Royal National Lifeboat Institution. These factual reports might be presented in the form of radio news flashes and interviews or the stories could be written up and read by children. The given notes merely suggest material which might be used.

Record: Storm sequence, *Four Sea Interludes: Peter Grimes.*

Narrator: When —— was at the seaside for a holiday, he saw the lifeboat launched.

Report: The boy might tell about the incident.

Narrator: The work of the Royal National Lifeboat Institution has been helped by children all over Britain, who shared in the *Blue Peter* collection of paperback books, which helped to buy four lifeboats. The work they do is varied.

Story: The picnic which lasted all night.

On 31st August, 1970, two women and four children were landed on Chuirn Island. During the day the weather changed and the boat could not take them off. The island had no shelter; a lifeboat was sent out to rescue the picnickers. The wind was gale force 5 and the rain was squally; the coxswain could not get the lifeboat close to the jetty. He was ordered by radio telephone to fetch a boarding boat from Port Askaig. The stranded children sheltered behind the lighthouse until the lifeboat returned. Two men volunteered to man the boarding boat and a searchlight was used to give them light. Second Coxswain Mackay carried the children down the rocky shore and into the boarding boat. By 6.30 a.m. they were all on the lifeboat, wrapped in warm blankets and sipping hot drinks.

Narrator: The lifeboat men do impossible things to help ships in distress. One of the best remembered stories is about an adventure which took place in January 1899.

Story: The Lynmouth lifeboat.

A big ship, the *Forrest Hall,* was in difficulties in the bay, but the strong westerly gale made it impossible to get the lifeboat out of the harbour. Coxswain John Crocombe thought that Porlock Bay might be calmer. The whole town turned out to help; twenty horses were harnessed to the boat's launching base. The lifeboat was hauled up Countisbury Hill, across the moor and down Porlock Hill (gradients of 1 in 4). The journey took all night but the lifeboat was launched from Porlock and the *Forrest Hall* was brought safely to port.

Narrator: Every time we hear radio announcements of gale warnings we should think of the lifeboat men who go into danger to save the lives of others.

Looking Forward to Easter

HOLIDAYS USUALLY begin in the middle of Holy Week, but there is value in taking an Assembly theme which anticipates the events which the Christian church remembers at this time. Each class may approach Easter in a different way, depending both on the age of the children and the inclination of their teachers; these Assemblies should reflect the work which has been done.

Processions and presents

Against a background reading of Mark 11: 7–10, the younger children could mime the triumphal entry scene and sing *Here comes Jesus riding on a donkey* or another hymn learnt in their Infants' classes.

A second procession might recall the Royal Maundy event, with one child dressed as a monarch, others representing the clergy, the Yeomen of the Guard and the recipients of the purses. The teacher or group spokesman should say something about the event. Read or tell a story based on the narrative in John 13: 3–9, 12–15, which lies behind the English custom.

A prayer might be built up using suggestions made by the children.

Or the leader may prefer to use a traditional prayer, saying something about the author,

e.g.   Thanks be to thee, our Lord Jesus Christ
For all the benefits thou hast won for us
For all the pains and insults thou hast borne for us
O most merciful Redeemer
Friend and Brother
May we know thee more clearly
Love thee more dearly
And follow thee more nearly
Now and ever.
                     Richard of Chichester.

The death of a king

An older class which has talked about the events of Holy Week may use their own written words or chosen readings in a modern translation. *New World* is recommended. Each part of the story can be introduced visually by children bringing forward symbols, like the bag of money or the crown of thorns.

Reader: Mark 11: 7–10.

Song: *All glory, laud and honour* or *Hosanna Hey Sanna (Jesus Christ Superstar)*

Narrator: But the shouts for the king soon became shouts for his death.

Reader: Judas planned the arrest of the king (Mark 14: 10, 11).

Reader: His chance came in the garden (Mark 14: 43–46).

Reader: They brought this king to Pilate (Mark 15: 1–3, 12, 13).

Reader: Soldiers mocked the king (Mark 15: 16–18).

Song: *Gentle Christ, wise and good,* vv. 1, 8, 9.

Reader: A stranger carried the cross for the king (Mark 15: 21, 22, 24).

Reader: A sign was put over the king's head (Mark 15: 26).

Song: *Gentle Christ, wise and good,* vv. 10, 11.

Reader: So the king died (Mark 15: 37, 39).

Reader: And just before sunset the king was put in a tomb (Mark 15: 42, 43, 46).

Narrator: But the story of the king goes on.

Song: *There on the hill a man is dying.*

The joy of Easter

There is no theme more difficult to tackle with a large company of children. Some teachers will want to use the traditional narratives; others will prefer to concentrate on the secular celebrations of Easter. It is clear that mature understanding of the Easter message will only come much later and, even then, only for some young people, but there is no reason why some part of it may not be imaginatively shared and emotionally felt at the Junior stage.

It might be worthwhile to ask one group of children to build up a mime sequence to accompany the first part of the narrative given below. Music could form a continuous background to the spoken word, perhaps an improvisation on the hymn tune which links together the death of the king (the theme of the second Assembly) and the joy of his Easter presence.

Song: *There on the hill a man is dying,* v. 1.

Narrator 1: It was dark when the women set out for the garden. Their eyes were red, for they had been crying. Without Jesus life seemed empty.

Narrator 2: It was dark when Peter came to the tomb. His eyes were sad; he knew that he had let Jesus down. Without Jesus life seemed empty.

Narrator 3: The two disciples were gloomy as they walked to Emmaus. Nothing could ever be the same again. Without Jesus life seemed empty.

Song: *There in the garden light is breaking,* v. 2 of above.

Narrator 1: There are several stories of the first Easter day. No one knows exactly what happened so long ago, but everyone knows that Easter is a happy time, a day of light and joy after days of darkness and sadness.

Narrator 2: So Easter is a time when church bells ring a glad message of joy.

Record: *Church bells.*

Narrator 3: And Easter is a time when spring flowers are used to decorate homes and churches, bringing light and joy after the darkness of winter.

Action: Children bring vases of flowers to decorate hall tables.

Narrator 1: Easter is a time when candles are lit, for joy and light has come to the world after the sadness and darkness of Good Friday.

Action: Candles are brought to the tables and lit.

Poem: The world itself keeps Easter Day,
And Easter larks are singing;
And Easter flowers are blooming gay,
And Easter buds are springing;
   Alleluya, Alleluya;
The Lord of all things lives anew,
And all his works are rising too.
J. M. Neale

Song: *Sing a glad song to Christ the King.*

Think of a World without . . .

THE HYMN which begins with these words has proved to be one of the most popular new songs of the seventies. Each verse might provide an opportunity for appreciating some aspect of creative life, in the world of nature and in the worlds of the arts and of scientific discovery.

Colour

Show paintings by children in the youngest class to introduce the fun we have with colour, comment on the experimental psychedelic patterning on some London buses or on the effectiveness of colour television in helping us to identify the beautiful things we see. Read Christina Rossetti's poem *What is Pink?* Build up a prayer with phrases suggested by the children and the sung or spoken repetition of the last line of the hymn, *We thank you, Lord, and praise your holy name.*

Introduce the third verse of the hymn, *Think of a world,* and link with the story of an artist whose pictures are known to the children. The story of Giotto is given as an example.

'Bare walls,' cried the apprentice, turning up his nose. 'Wait!' said the master painter. 'The walls are not going to be bare for long. Signor Enrico Scrovegni has asked me to paint frescoes for these chapel walls. You will be helping me, mixing the paint and moving the ladder.' The boy apologised for his hasty speech.

'Look at my design,' said Giotto the master painter, unrolling his papers. 'See! Here are pictures to tell a story. See! Here on that bare south wall we shall put pictures of the young Jesus. Below them we'll paint pictures showing the last week in his life.' The boy stared at the drawings. 'I know that story well,' he exclaimed, as he pointed his finger at a sketch of Judas kissing Jesus. 'What a traitor he was.' As they looked at the pictures, the boy began to see how the bare walls would come alive with colour and story. 'When shall we begin work?'

Today, visitors from all over the world stare at the plain outside walls of the Arena Chapel in Padua. Then they go inside and see the great coloured paintings with which Giotto covered the bare walls five hundred years ago.

An imagined scene based on the work of Giotto.

Exploration and discovery

Remind the children of a recent space expedition or a news item of scientific significance; this might be done with the help of colour slides (e.g. the Woodmansterne set on Apollo 15) or the poster *Moon Walk*. Use the children's knowledge to build up a roll of honour of those whose discoveries have benefited man or whose expeditions have taken them to unknown parts of the universe (e.g. Edmund Hillary and Sherpa Tenzing, first men to reach the summit of Mount Everest; Christiaan Barnard, surgeon who has tried to replace damaged hearts; or Neil Armstrong, first man to set foot on the moon).

Select readings or stories which tell of men's excitement at their discovery, their awe in the face of scientific or natural wonders or the dangers they meet during their journeys. These might include part of Gen. 1, read by Frank Borman, Jim Lovell and Bill Anders on Apollo mission 8 as the spacecraft circled the moon at Christmas 1968, the story of Vasco Nunez de Balboa, sighting the Pacific Ocean after travelling across the Panama Isthmus in 1513 and kneeling to give thanks for the privilege of making the discovery, Captain Oates' sacrifice in his attempt to lessen the burden for his friends in the Antarctic expedition of 1912, linking with the appropriate verse of *Think of a world*.

End with the prayer of Sir Francis Drake, another explorer and adventurer:

O Lord God, when Thou givest us Thy servants to endeavour any great matter, grant us also to know that it is not the beginning, but the continuing of the same until it be thoroughly finished, which yieldeth the true glory; through Him who for the finishing of Thy work laid down His life.

Family and friends

Use Oxfam home pictures from different parts of the world, family situation illustrations (e.g. parent reading to child, a meal together) as the focal point for Assembly, or suggest the lines of the hymn verse by displaying a frieze of a street of houses.

Narrator: A bed at night, breakfast on the table, a carpet on the floor, pocket-money to spend—we take these things for granted.

Child 1: Someone to mend our clothes.

Child 2: Someone to cook our meals.

Child 3: Someone to talk to before we go to bed.

Narrator: Mothers, fathers, grandparents, aunts—we take these people for granted. Let us give thanks for our homes and families. (Silence)
Robert Herrick wrote a poem of thanksgiving for his home.

Reader: Lord, Thou hast given me a cell
    Wherein to dwell:
A little house, whose humble roof
    Is weather-proof;
Under the spars of which I lie
    Both soft and dry. . . .
Some brittle sticks of thorn or briar
    Make me a fire,
Close by whose living coal I sit,
    And glow like it . . .
Thou mak'st my teeming hen to lay
    Her egg each day. . . .
All these, and better Thou dost send
    Me, to this end,
That I should render, for my part,
    A thankful heart.
            Robert Herrick.

Narrator:	Think of a town without any houses . . . it seems a stupid thing to say.
Child 1:	But when a hurricane hit Pennsylvania many homes were destroyed.
Child 2:	When there was war in Pakistan, many homes were burnt down.
Child 3:	When there was an earthquake in Turkey, homes disappeared under the rubble.
Narrator:	Then friendly people from all over the world joined together to help.
Teacher 1:	Tents and blankets were sent for the homeless.
Action:	Children set up a tent or huddle in blankets.
Teacher 2:	Lorries arrived with materials for building new houses.
Action:	Mime of building operations and families moving in.
Narrator:	These gifts came from people who were grateful for their own homes and who wanted to show their friendship to those without homes.
Song:	*Think of a world,* v. 6.
Narrator:	We are grateful for the friends we have. Mr. Green helps to coach our school football team on Saturday mornings. Mrs. Everitt stands at the crossing to stop the traffic for children coming to school . . . Friends help, friends care, friends are loyal to one another.
Story:	Tell the story of a famous friendship (e.g. David and Jonathan, based on 1 Sam. 18: 3–9; 19: 1–12; 20: 1–23, 35–42).
Song:	*Father we thank thee for the night.*

It's Worth a Fight

A STUDENT using Oxfam materials on her final teaching practice found a ready sympathy for needy children and an eagerness to plan a concert and display in aid of the charity. A teacher working with nine year olds on the theme *Helping Hands* realised their interest in the stories of those who have championed the cause of people in need. The phenomenal success of *Blue Peter* appeals shows how Primary and Middle school children vigorously support causes.

Enthusiasm for helping may be short-lived but, if children are capable of recognising and responding to a need, opportunity should be given for them to collect information about charities and social pioneers and to find ways of helping others in their locality or more distant places. The Assembly themes may relate to such work, being a culminating point for one class and an opening of the door of concern for other classes.

The fight against hunger

With introductory sentences for each section, present a movement sequence based on ideas developed in class:

a. The farmer digs up his vegetable patch, while his wife pounds the manioc. His children reach out eager hands for food, but there never seems to be sufficient.

b. Agricultural experts come to the village and the men gather round. Some reject modern ideas; others work hard for a while, and then slacken their effort.

c. Encouraged by his hungry children, one farmer perseveres.

d. The farmer and his children gather the crop and go home in triumphant procession with agricultural experts and villagers.

Information about agricultural projects can be reported by members of the class,

e.g. *War on Want* collected 2,361,280 Green Shield stamps to send a tractor and plough to Botswana;

Christian Aid says that five new pence will buy one baby chicken for Brazil.

Sing *We must help the poor and needy*; use a prayer of concern made up by one of the children.

The fight against blindness

Organise a picture display (e.g. a guide dog with her harness) and an exhibition of mechanical aids for the blind (e.g. an iron with Braille markings). In a small school this display may be the focal point of the Assembly itself; in larger schools invite classes to see the exhibition before the Assembly begins.

Children might read prepared statements about those who refused to accept their blindness as a handicap, using material from newspapers and stories of famous people,

e.g. Louis Braille never saw the alphabet he invented, but thousands of blind people can read through their finger-tips because of his invention;

Blind Jack of Knaresborough, John Metcalf, could not see the roads on which he walked, but he led a campaign for the improvement of roads in England;

Blind Chris Cornell set out to ride on horseback from John O'Groats to Land's End to raise money for a home and training centre for blind and disabled people.

Better still would be the visit of a blind person to the school to talk briefly about his achievements.

Sing verses from *Let us with a gladsome mind*, written by John Milton, who became blind later in his life.

The fight for health

Older children might develop such a theme by considering how people in the past fought disease, how recent discoveries have helped to control some deficiency diseases and how preventive work is encouraged in the developing countries. The Assembly would bring together elements of their study. If possible, practical work should be displayed (e.g. a mural of the Eyam villagers) with teaching aids (e.g. the Florence Nightingale poster issued by the Post Office Postal Publicity Branch and *The world-wide fight against malaria* picture from the *Themes in Religious Education* set 2 collection). The readings introducing each section and the Ronald Ross poem should be read by a teacher.

Teacher: Today we think about the fight to bring health to the peoples of the world. All through the ages men have tried to discover how to conquer dreaded diseases.

Reader 1: Long ago, many people died from the plague, which spread quickly from place to place.

Reader 2: A London tailor sent a box of clothes to the village of Eyam in Derbyshire. It was 1665, the year of the Great Plague. The man who unpacked the box was the first to die of the fever; then others were taken ill. William Mompesson, rector of the village, suggested a plan to the frightened villagers.

Reader 3: 'We must cut ourselves off from the outside world. This is the only way to stop the plague from spreading to other villages.'

Reader 4: Brave men like William Mompesson and the Eyam villagers helped to conquer the dreaded plague.

Teacher: Through the ages women have tried to get better standards of nursing care.

Dramatisation: The scene might be Florence Nightingale confronting Dr. John Hall in the Crimea.

Reader 5:	Brave women like Florence Nightingale have helped to relieve suffering and to make people well.
Song:	*Sweet Polly Oliver* (sung by a group).
Teacher:	Through the ages scientists have tried to discover the sources of infection and the ways in which disease can be conquered.
Reader 6:	Ronald Ross knew that there must be a way of beating malaria, which caused the death of millions of people. At last, he proved that the dapple-winged mosquito was a carrier of malaria.
Reader 7:	That night he wrote some verses and put them in a letter to his wife.
Teacher:	This day, relenting God Hath placed within my hand A wondrous thing: and God Be praised. At his command Seeking his secret deeds With tears and toiling breath, I find thy cunning seeds, O million-murdering Death.
Reader 8:	Let us give thanks for those men and women who have helped in the fight for health.

Prayer:	We remember that Florence Nightingale and her nurses fought to get proper medical treatment for soldiers in the Crimea
	    And give thanks for the love they showed.
	We remember that Ronald Ross and his friends gave long years to research into the causes of malaria
	    And give thanks for the love they showed.
	We remember that Alexander Fleming found the value of penicillin and that Edward Jenner discovered the power of vaccination
	    And give thanks for the love they showed.

Food, Glorious Food

'ANOTHER egg sandwich please!' '*Another* one?' Many Juniors eat enormously and with enjoyment. They think that the larders' supplies are boundless and give little thought that their surreptitious extraction of a cake may throw out the calculations for a family tea. Thanks for food may be easily expressed; shock tactics may be necessary to arouse the imagination sufficiently to understand the plight of the world's hungry.

It may be appropriate to have the detailed harvest thanksgiving theme, *Celebrating Harvest*, early in the week and to consider the needs of others on subsequent days. In many schools, work on this theme will lead to a practical expression of concern.

The cupboard is bare

Arouse the children's awareness of the sharp contrast in food supplies by comparing the daily menu of an English child, amounting to something like 2,000 calories, with that of a child in South-east Asia, where a diet of rice, vegetables and a little fish might amount to 900 calories per day. This might be done with the help of actual platefuls of food and a graph. Use pictures (e.g. Oxfam's *Hunger: Causes and Solutions*, Freedom from Hunger's *Help for Self Help*) to comment on the causes of malnutrition and inadequate food supplies. Read or sing *Now join we to praise the Creator*.

Tell a story which suggests that this is an age-old problem. Teachers who wish to use a biblical illustration might choose the one about Joseph, the comptroller of the granaries for a Pharoah of Egypt (Gen. 41: 29–49, 53–57; 42: 1–7) or the story of Ruth the gleaner (Ruth 2: 1–23). Those who have classes working on life in earlier times in England might choose the story of Wilfrid.

> When he went to preach to the south Saxons in A.D. 681, he found that people were starving, unaware of the food resources of the sea nearby. He taught them to use boats and to make nets, so that they might catch food for themselves.

Finish with a time of quiet thinking, linked with such words as:

Our supermarkets are full of food
while half the world is hungry.
May we remember those whose cupboards are bare.
Food we cannot eat goes into the dustbin
while half the world is hungry.
May we remember those who do not get enough to eat.
We turn up our noses if we get the same foods too often
while half the world is hungry.
May we remember those who seldom get anything but the cheapest and most filling food.
Someone must help the hungry.
Let us find ways of helping.

Food for the world

During this Assembly it may be desirable to highlight the work of one charity concerned with world food provisions, perhaps a charity which is already supported by the school. Alternatively it may be thought best to tell short stories about different kinds of aid which are given for short and long term relief.

Play a recording of *Food, Glorious Food* and recall the closing words of the previous Assembly. Use filmstrip, slides or pictures from one of the charities to highlight the stories told.

> The women stood near the drilling rig, their brass water pots on their lips. Good drinking water, plenty of water for washing, no more walking three miles to the nearest well—it seemed like a dream. The men patiently waited while the headman of the village stepped forward to work the new pump fitted on their new well. Cyrus Gaikwad looked on in satisfaction as the water began to flow; he uses machines and explosives provided by Christian Aid to help the farmers and women of India.

Those who choose to concentrate on one agency might use an Oxfam wallet, *India: Country and People*, which provides pictures on food production and preparation, a gramophone record and a game appropriate for sharing at Assembly. Other material for this theme is given in *Food—1 & 2*, in worship leaflets from Christian Aid and reports from the Save The Children Fund.

Celebrating harvest

Each section of the Assembly might be taken by a different class, with a connecting narrative planned by a teacher. The following outline is based on the various harvest projects attempted in one school. Its contents reflect the particular religious backgrounds of the children there.

Narrator: At this time of the year we remember the good things we have to eat.

Action: Children bring forward representative harvest gifts, saying what it is they are carrying and from what country it comes.

Choral speaking:

A. Harvest of orchards
All over the world.
A1. Crisp, juicy apples
A2. Mellow, ripe pears
A1. Oranges, lemons
A2. Purple red plums.
A. These are the fruits of men's work through the year.
B. Harvest of hedgerows
Along country lanes.
B1. Plump little blackberries
To make into jam.
B2 Hazel nuts brown
For squirrels to hide.
B1. Rowan and elder
To feed hungry birds.
B. High on the hedgerow,
There for the picking
Fruits of the countryside
Generously growing.

Narrator: At this time of the year farmers and their families used to join in the fun of harvest home.

Action:	A country dance, or show corn dollies and a model of harvest time in the past.
Song:	*The combines have lumbered through fields of wheat* or *When oats and corn have ripened.*
Narrator:	At this time of the year Jewish families celebrate the feast of Succoth.
Dramatisation:	Use screens as a booth, providing twig branches to go over the top and fruit to hang from the branches. *Father:* Long ago every Jewish family would have a booth near the house. They fetched branches to make a booth like this. *Son:* Why do you leave a space between the branches? *Father:* We look through the branches and see the stars in the sky. They remind us of the days and nights when the Jews wandered in a desert place and slept in tents. As they looked up into the night sky, they felt that God was near, caring for them on their long journey. *Mother:* Here is some fruit, Reuben. Hang it from the branches. *Son:* Why do we put fruit in the booth? *Mother:* The fruit reminds us of the gifts we enjoy at harvest and of the days when the Jewish people first settled in the promised land and learnt how to grow crops.
Reading:	Levit. 23: 39–43.
Record:	Israeli harvesting song—hakotskrim.

Trees

In BUILDING a new London school men using the bulldozers were careful to avoid damaging the solitary tree which stood in the middle of the former slum clearance area. That tree will continue to give pleasure to the children who sit in its shade during hot summer dinner hours and will provide an illusion of 'country air' in a brick wilderness. Out of such common stuff may grow an expression of thanks.

Protest

Give a summary of the story of *The Latchkey Children*, written by Eric Allen, and read a passage from the book, possibly part of chapter 13. If the story is already well known in the school, it may be appropriate for a group of children to interpret the ideas in a mime sequence, to which a brief commentary is added. The sequence might follow this pattern:

a. Children playing and fighting round their tree.
b. March of the planners, to measure and chalk out the position of the concrete engine (chap. 3).
c. Children getting lost in County Hall, handed from one official to another, and getting no positive response (chap. 7).
d. Seeing the children's dejection, one of the workmen refuses to hack at the tree (chap. 13).
e. The children dance triumphantly beside the tree they have saved.

The beauty of trees

If the Assembly is held indoors, use silhouettes or pictures to feature different tree shapes and to talk about their fruits and leaf patterns. Link with poems, e.g. *A Child's Song in Spring*, E. Nesbit, *Trees*, Walter de la Mare, or Sara Coleridge's poem with the same title:

> The Oak is called the King of Trees,
> The Aspen quivers in the breeze,

The Poplar grows up straight and tall,
The Pear tree spreads along the wall,
The Sycamore gives pleasant shade,
The Willow droops in watery glade,
The Fir tree useful timber gives,
The Beech amid the forest lives.

Children in one class might prepare beforehand a frieze to illustrate
words from Psalm 104: 16, 17, 20–23 (NEB), given below, including
woodcutters as well as trees and animals.

The trees of the Lord are green and leafy,
the cedars of Lebanon which he planted;
the birds build their nests in them,
the stork makes her home in their tops . . . .
When thou makest darkness and it is night,
all the beasts of the forest come forth;
the young lions roar for prey
seeking for food from God.
When thou makest the sun rise, they slink away
and go to rest in their lairs;
but man comes out to his work
and to his labours until evening.

Sing *For air and sunshine, pure and sweet*, vv. 1, 2.

At a suitable time of the year, this Assembly might be held in the play-
ground, if there are trees there. At blossom time, A. E. Housman's poem
Loveliest of Trees, would be suitable. Alternatively, a tree-planting cere-
mony might take place, in the presence of members of the Parent-
Teacher Association, if they have subscribed funds for growing plants and
shrubs.

The usefulness of trees

On an expedition children may have been able to collect leaves and tree fruits, take bark rubbings, carve a piece of wood or make a floral decoration with an interesting bark shape and wild plants. Use such work as reference points for the Assembly's detailed planning.

Focal point 1: Wooden spoon, cheese board.

Narrator: A bread board, baking spoons—in our homes wood plays its useful part. So we give thanks for the wood which is used in the home.

Pause:

Focal Point 2: Paper and bark.

Narrator: Mother wants to write a letter? Fetch her a piece of paper. John wants to make a dart? Find a piece of paper. Every day millions of tons of paper are used, and paper is made from wood pulp.

Story: The Birch Bark Talks.

'I want these Cree Indians to read the Bible for themselves,' said James Evans. It sounded easy enough, but the Cree Indians had no written language. So James Evans had to make up a Cree alphabet before he could begin the job of translating the Bible into the Cree language.

When that was finished, there was another problem. No paper, no ink! 'What shall I do now?' thought James Evans. The Indians came forward with an idea. They took the soft lining of the birch tree's bark, pressed and dried it, until it made a rough sort of paper. But what about ink? Soot and fish oil were mixed together. At last James Evans could get his translation of the Bible story written down.

Then the Indians clamoured for reading lessons so that they could read for themselves the story written on birch bark.

Narrator:	So we give thanks for the wood which makes paper for books.
Pause:	
Focal point 3:	A wooden doll, bricks.
Narrator:	Long before the days of plastic, children had games and toys made of wood, dolls, jigsaw puzzles, bats and tops. So we give thanks for the wood which makes toys.
Pause:	
Focal point 4:	A carpenter's tools.
Narrator:	Window frames and doors—our houses depend on the work of the carpenter. Carvings for the mantelpiece—the work of another expert in wood. (At this point a carpenter might talk to the children.) So we give thanks for the usefulness of wood in building houses and boats, and for the beauty of carved pictures and shapes.
Pause:	
Focal point 5:	Picture of a shady tree or a forest.
Reading:	Psalm 104: 16, 17, 20–23.
Narrator:	So we give thanks for the life of the forest, for the shade of a tree in the park, and for those who work in the woods.
Song:	*All things bright and beautiful.*

Follow my Leader

THE CHILD in the Primary school has a tremendous enthusiasm for some hero of the moment, a footballer, a leading horsewoman or a pop-singer. The boy decorates the bedroom walls with pictures of his hero; the girl hangs around to get the autograph of hers; both try to copy the way of life adopted by their hero, even down to clothes. More important and more indirectly, the values of the hero become their own. Such enthusiasm may be used as a lead-in to the Assembly theme.

Biographical material has long had its place in programmes of religious education and there may be an opportunity to serialise the story of some-one who has followed the leader of his choice. An example from the past is used here as an illustration; contemporary figures should be used where possible.

Off to Labrador

If a teacher presents the theme, slides borrowed from the Grenfell Association would build up an understanding of the conditions of life and work in Labrador. Material from the Commonwealth Institute may be found suitable.

Begin with choral speaking:

Girls: Treacherous currents
Jagged cliffs
The coast of Labrador.

Boys: Baffling fog
Ice-patched sea
The coast of Labrador.

Girls: Frozen spray
Swirling waves
The coast of Labrador.

Boys: Scattered villages
Cut off by blizzards
The coast of Labrador.

The children might be able to suggest the sort of injury likely to be suffered in such an area, i.e. frost-bite, starvation, men mauled by wild animals, men injured on the ice pans. Tell the story of one occasion when Dr. Wilfred Grenfell was able to help.

'Doctor, can you help?' The two men stood on the doctor's doorstep, covered in snow. It was a terrible night and the men looked exhausted. 'Who wants me?' asked the doctor. 'Uncle Lige at Wild Bight Bay,' was their reply. No wonder the men were exhausted—they had made a journey of one hundred miles through a snow blizzard to reach Dr. Grenfell.

It took the three men four days to get to Wild Bight Bay, going as fast as they could through the blizzard during the day, huddling close to one another and to the dogs at night. At last one cried, 'There's the cottage.' To reach it they had to swing from tree to tree down a precipice. Once there, Dr. Grenfell was able to give Uncle Lige the treatment he needed.

Follow up the story with the comment once made by Dr. Grenfell: 'The tough jobs are the ones which appeal to real men.'

Caring about children
Build up a wall board with pictures brought by the children showing the care that is given to youngsters, and add a list of names, again supplied by the children, of those who have given special thought to their needs. Some teachers may wish to link this with a reading of Mark 10: 13–16 and a song like *It fell upon a summer's day*.
Dramatise a scene showing how Dr. Grenfell's care of children began.

The doctor and his two young companions went into a hut which seemed to be empty. There they found four starving children. A woman carrying a baby returned to the hut with the berries she had collected as food for the children. She asked the doctor to take the children and care for them, since she was no longer able to do so. The young men took off their coats to wrap round the children before carrying them away.

Sing *Kum ba yah* with interjections between verses, using illustrations given by the children,

e.g. Someone's hungry, Lord . . .
Dr. Grenfell found homes and food for children who were starving.
Someone's dying, Lord . . .
Dr. Barnardo took in children who had lost their parents.

Real adventure

If slides were borrowed for this week make use of selected frames to recall the Labrador setting and the work of Dr. Grenfell.

Choral
speaking: Mile after mile
Over hummocky snow
Across frozen waves
Of ice-locked bays
Dog-teams bumped
Strained and slithered
Pulling the sledge.
A tough life
A rough life
Dr. Grenfell's life
In Labrador.

Narrator: Life for Dr. Grenfell was full of adventure. There was an occasion when he nearly lost his own life in his attempts to save life.

Story: On the ice pan.

'Doctor, you are urgently needed sixty miles away.' On Easter Sunday, 1908, Grenfell got this message and harnessed his dog team. The ice was beginning to break up; the snow was getting soft; it would not be an easy journey. Hoping to save time Grenfell took a short cut across a frozen sea bay, but the ice began to break and he had to swim for his life to reach an ice pan as his sledge sank. Fortunately he had time to cut the dogs' harness, but then he only survived the freezing night by killing three dogs to make himself a skin coat. He hoisted a flag made of dog bones and his frozen shirt and was spotted by fishermen who rescued him.

Narrator: Dr. Grenfell once said: 'To follow Jesus—I believe that this is the only real adventure of life.'
Jesus once said: 'Anyone who wishes to be a follower of mine must leave self behind.' (Mark 8: 34, NEB.)

Silence:

Song: *Fisherman Peter on the sea,* with additional verse about Grenfell or *Thou perfect hero knight.*

Prayer: Teach us, good Lord,
To serve Thee as Thou deservest
To give, and not to count the cost
To fight, and not to heed the wounds
To toil, and not to seek for rest
To labour, and not to ask for any reward
Save that of knowing that we do Thy will.

Tales of Long Ago

ALL THROUGH the ages men have told stories which attempt to answer the basic questions of existence—Who am I? What am I here for? How did the world come into being? Most of these stories were written before man had the scientific knowledge of the nature of the universe which is accepted today. Nevertheless, such stories are worth sharing, for many of them convey a sense of thanksgiving for the wonders of the universe and can prompt the children's wonder and an awareness of man's responsibility for all living things.

The coming of light

Tell the Mexican myth of the gods' gift or indicate sufficient of its content to provide a background for watchers while other children present a movement sequence based on this story. Use simple costume or masks to distinguish the gods of light from the rest of the group. The pattern of movement might be as follows:

Narration: The world was in complete darkness.

Movement: People groping about, falling over rocks, stumbling into pools of water, hearing frightening noises.

Narration: Because there was no light, there was no warmth.

Movement: People shivering with cold, huddling together.

Narration: The gods looked at its misery and decided to give light to the world they had made.

Movement: Gods come to watch the people as they grope in the dark gloom. When the gods sit round a fire the people move tentatively closer, stretching out their hands to the blaze. Two gods step out to give light.

Narration: But the light was too bright.

Movement: People, dazzled by the glare, hide their faces; children are overcome by the heat.

Narration: So the gods commanded the wind to blow the sun away for a while.

Movement: The wind sends the sun into the distance, the moon shines alone. People sleep in its gentler light and, as the sun returns, people get up to go to their work.

Narration: So the pattern of day and night was made, says the old Mexican story, and the gods saw that this was good.

Sing a song of thanksgiving for the sun and moon, possibly one made up by children or *Praise, O praise our God and King*.

Fire so bright

Provide pictures as talking points, e.g. a family round a coal or gas fire, a steelworks, the Olympic torch, a bonfire, Scouts cooking out-of-doors. Put the question, 'How did we first get fire?', in a story setting (e.g. children enjoying their camp fire at a school camp) and tell the Prometheus myth as one example of the answers given by people long ago.

> Prometheus took handfuls of clay and kneaded them with water to make men. He and his brother, Epimetheus, discussed how they might make men stronger and greater than the other animals. Prometheus suggested that men should be given something from heaven, which was beyond the reach of other living creatures, so he stole fire from the wheel of the sun chariot as it passed over the horizon. He brought the fire back to Greece for men's use.

Children might read statements about the things men could do when they first got fire,
e.g. with fire, men could make weapons to protect them from wild animals;
with fire, men could keep themselves warm:
with fire, men could bake the cooking pots they made from clay.

Suggest that Francis of Assisi had another way of giving thanks for fire and sing his hymn, *All creatures of our God and king*, vv. 1–3.

73

Living things

Narrator: About 2,500 years ago another story about the beginning of the world was written down. Through its words we give thanks for the things we enjoy on the land and in the water.

Reading: God said, 'Let the earth put forth vegetation, plants yielding seed, and fruit trees bearing fruit . . .' And it was so. (Gen. 1: 11, RSV.)

Narrator: Let us give thanks for flowers and trees.

Focal point: A frieze of growing plant life prepared by a younger class. Use whatever illustration and poem is appropriate to the season in the following way:

Narrator: 'Look at those daffodils,' exclaimed Dorothy Wordsworth to her brother, as they walked beside the lake, one windy day in April. The flowers looked so beautiful that the Wordsworths could only stand and stare. Later William Wordsworth wrote a poem about those daffodils.

Poem: I wandered lonely as a cloud
That floats on high o'er vales and hills;
When all at once I saw a crowd,
A host, of golden daffodils;
Beside the lake, beneath the trees,
Fluttering and dancing in the breeze.

Reading: God said, 'Let the waters bring forth swarms of living creatures, and let birds fly above the earth . . .' And it was so. (Gen. 1: 20, RSV.)

Narrator: Let us give thanks for the birds.

Record: *Sounds of the Countryside* (excerpt).

74

Reading: God said, 'Let the earth bring forth living creatures . . . cattle and creeping things, and beasts of the earth . . .' And it was so. (Gen. 1: 24, RSV.)

Narrator: Let us give thanks for animals and reptiles, prehistoric monsters and the pets we own.

Riddles e.g. My tongue darts out to catch my food. My colour
prepared by changes as I move on to different things.
children:

Choral Slowly moving
reading: Dinosaurs
Clumsy creatures
Very long.
Scolosaurus
Armour-plated
Tyrannosaurus
Fierce and strong.

Reading: Then God said, 'Let us make man in our image . . . and let them have dominion over the fish of the sea, and over the birds of the air, and over the cattle, and over all the earth.' (Gen. 1: 26, RSV.)

Song: *To God who makes all lovely things.*

Prayer: Let us thank God for the lovely things in our world
for tall pine trees and shy violets.
Let us thank God for the gay things in our world
for dancing butterflies and the darting kingfisher.
Let us thank God for the lovely sounds in our world
for the crash of the sea and the song of the skylark.
Let us thank God for beautiful scents in our world
for the sweet smell of roses.
Let us thank God for the people in our world
those we meet and those far away.

Reading: The old Jewish story ends with these words:
And God saw everything that he had made, and behold, it was very good. (Gen. 1: 31, RSV.)

Achievement

IF WE REGARD the Assembly as a time for school family sharing and happiness, it should give us opportunities to be thankful for individual and group achievements. The theme might be introduced on a day when the head teacher is asked to distribute swimming certificates or when a music group is going to share in an inter-school festival.

By the time children come into the Junior school there is considerable rivalry amongst them, and some children begin to feel inadequate because they are not making obvious progress in things which some adults seem to regard as important. It may be an encouragement to such children to hear about those who have overcome initial handicaps and this element is suggested as part of the third Assembly.

Olympic style
Looking at a montage of sportsmen prepared by one of the classes and drawing on the children's observations about current favourites on the sports' field, say something along these lines:

> We are glad that television helps us to enjoy many sports.
> We are glad to see the skill of —— on the tennis court.
> We are glad to watch the pace of —— running at the stadium.
> We are glad to learn how footballers work together as a team.

Lead into conversation about sportsmanship and the importance of working as a team. This might be illustrated by a reading from *First Four Minutes*, in which Roger Bannister describes how his achievement was the result of his partnership with Christopher Brasher and Christopher Chataway.

Sing *Lord, I love to stamp and shout* or *For all the strength we have.*

Music for pleasure

Play *Doctor Gradus ad Parnassum*, the first piece in Debussy's *Children's Corner Suite*, telling the children about the content of the piece, written for his daughter Claude-Emma.

The young player starts her practice with enthusiasm, her fingers darting up and down the keyboard but, as her fingers tire, she loses interest and the music slows down. Thinking about the play-time she is missing, she plays badly, until she realises that the practice period is nearly over. Her playing gets more lively and she ends with triumphant thuds of defiance—that's over for today!

Invite children to play recorders, a piece they have composed for chime bars and percussion, or to sing a recently learnt song. Listen to an extract from *The Song of Hiawatha* (*H. W. Longfellow*):

> Two good friends had Hiawatha,
> Singled out from all the others . . .
> Chibiabos, the musician,
> And the very strong man, Kwasind.
> Most beloved by Hiawatha
> Was the gentle Chibiabos,
> He the best of all musicians,
> He the sweetest of all singers . . .
> When he sang, the village listened;
> All the warriors gathered round him,
> All the women came to hear him;
> Now he stirred their souls to passion,
> Now he melted them to pity . . .
> For he sang of peace and freedom,
> Sang of beauty, love and longing,
> Sang of death, and life undying
> In the Islands of the Blessed . . .
> Very dear to Hiawatha
> Was the gentle Chibiabos,
> He the best of all musicians,
> He the sweetest of all singers;
> For his gentleness he loved him,
> And the magic of his singing.

Sing *Thank you for every note of music* (v. 3 of *Thank you for waking me this morning*) or *Sing a glad song to Christ the King*.

It's not easy

Narrator: Climbing ropes, playing the recorder, running a race—none of these things is easy. The climber needs strong muscles; the recorder player needs good breath control; the runner needs long hours of training. One man may find life hard because he is shy. Another may find it difficult to achieve his ambition because he is poor. To-day's stories are about people who know how difficult it is to achieve success.

Story: Caedmon the herdsman.

Caedmon skipped out of the great hall when the harp was passed round after supper. He was too shy to take a turn at singing to entertain the company. One night he dreamt he could sing and he was persuaded to try out his voice and his song in front of the Abbess Hilda.

Dramatisation: A group might act the scene from *The Song of Caedmon*, in which he slowly sings his song and is then joined by the rest of the company (the school in this case). If this is not feasible, listen to the recording of Caedmon's song after the story.

Story: Lord Nuffield.

Bicycles made in a garden shed, car parts assembled in the back garden —this was the way William Richard Morris began his work. Later, as a successful businessman, he employed hundreds of men in his Cowley factory and Morris cars went on the roads of the world.

Narrator: William Richard Morris, Lord Nuffield, became a millionaire, but he shared much of his wealth with other people. He knew what life was like for a poor man, because he had been poor himself.

Focal point: Picture of Mount Everest.

Narrator: Climbing Everest has been the ambition of many moun-taineers. In 1953 two men reached the top for the first time, achieving success because of the team of moun-taineers who had worked with them. It was not easy, but they got there.

Reading: Edmund Hillary wrote:

'I was beginning to tire a little now. I had been cutting steps con-tinuously for two hours, and Tenzing, too, was moving very slowly. As I chipped steps round still another corner, I wondered rather dully just how long we could keep it up. Our original zest had now quite gone and it was turning more into a grim struggle. I then realised that the ridge ahead, instead of monotonously rising, now dipped sharply away, and far below I could see the North Col and the Rongbuk glacier. I looked upwards to see a narrow snow ridge running up to a snowy summit. A few more whacks of the ice-axe in the firm snow and we stood on top.'

Extract from *The Ascent of Everest* by John Hunt

Song: *Lord I love to stamp and shout*

Prayer: Trying hard
Practising carefully
Working as a team
Help us make every effort to achieve success in the things we do.

The Freedom Road

THE CONCEPT of freedom will be understood by Juniors only in practical terms, but looking at the theme now may provide a ground for later understanding at other levels. The older children who prepare the movement sequences are obviously likely to grasp more of its significance than the younger ones. All of them may appreciate the stories of those who, through courageous effort, have won freedom for themselves and others.

If the school has a considerable number of Jewish children, the second day provides a chance for them to describe the Passover tradition; in other circumstances it would be more appropriate to choose another aspect of the theme.

Escape

Two groups of children might mime a scene in which refugees try to evade searching soldiers, possibly using a choral chant as a background to the scene.

The road is dark	The road is dark
They hurry along	They march along
No time to rest	Loud is the beat
No time for food.	Of soldiers' feet.
Freedom, freedom	Look for the traitors!
This is their need.	Bring them to justice!
Children stumble	Search the woods
Babies cry.	Patrol the rivers.
Hurry! Hurry!	March them away
We dare not stop.	Their day is done.

The road is dark
They creep along.
No time to weep
No time to rest.
Freedom, freedom
This is their goal.

Alternatively, tell the story of Gladys Aylward and the march of one hundred children across the mountains. A prayer along these lines is indicated:

> We remember those who suffer in time of war
> Children who lose their homes
> Families broken up and separated
> People who lose their belongings
> And those who lose their country.
> We remember those who help the victims of war
> The Red Cross
> The Pestalozzi Children's Villages.

Remembering a great escape
Give a brief introduction to the Passover event and set a Seder table with its traditional food elements (i.e. lamb bone, egg, grated horse-radish, lettuce, haroset and matzah). As children bring forward these foods they should say something about the historical significance of each element.

e.g. We eat these bitter herbs to remind us of the bitter life of our ancestors in Egypt (Ex. 1: 13, 14).

This is the unleavened bread which reminds us that our ancestors left Egypt in a hurry, before the dough had time to rise (Ex. 12: 39).

Or the matzah may be brought forward with the words of the ancient litany:

This is the bread of affliction that our fathers ate in the land of Egypt. All who are hungry, let them come and eat. All who are needy, let them come and celebrate Passover with us. Now we are here; next year may we be in Israel. Now we are slaves; in the year ahead may we be free men.

One of the children might ask the question, 'Why is this night different from all other nights?' to be answered by the reading of Deut. 26: 5-8.

Use the following prayer:

> Thanks be to God.
> He brought us from slavery to freedom,
> > from sorrow to joy,
> > from darkness to light.
> Thanks be to God.

It may be appropriate to play a Jewish folk song at the end of Assembly, such as *Let us all be merry* from *Raisins and Almonds*.

Let my people go

Slave trade posters may be prepared by a class working on this theme.

Dramatisation: The arrival and sale of slaves.

Song: *Go down, Moses.*

Narrator: That song, telling a story of long ago, became the theme song of the slaves in America. It was so popular that slave owners banned it. But still the singing went on; the slaves looked forward to the day of freedom. The song became a password, used on the underground railroad.

Story: The underground railroad.

Harriet Tubman discovered that it was not a railroad at all, but a chain of people willing to help slaves to escape to the 'free' northern states in America. Knowing that the penalty of imprisonment or a fine might result from helping the fugitive slaves, she became a 'conductor' on the railroad after her own escape along this route. She led over 300 people from slavery to freedom.

Song: *Go down, Moses.*

Narrator: Whilst Harriet Tubman was working for other slaves in America, Lord Shaftesbury in England was trying to free children who were slaves in factories and mines.

Poem with movement: *The Cry of the Children.*

For, all day, we drag our burden tiring
    Through the coal-dark underground.
Or, all day, we drive the wheels of iron
    In the factories, round and round.
For all day the wheels are droning, turning;
    Their wind comes in our faces,
Till our hearts burn, our heads with pulses burning,
    And the walls turn in their places;
Turns the sky in the high window, blank and reeling,
    Turns the long light that drops adown the wall,
Turns the black flies that crawl along the ceiling.
    All are turning, all the day, and we with all,
And all the day, the iron wheels are droning,
    And sometimes we could pray
'O ye wheels' (breaking out in a mad moaning)
    'Stop! Be silent for today!'
                    Elizabeth Barrett Browning.

Narrator: For thousands of children imprisoned among the wheels
of factory and mine, Lord Shaftesbury gained freedom.
But still there are those who look for freedom, freedom
from hunger, freedom from fear, freedom of worship. . . .
Another song has become the theme song of those looking
for freedom.

Song: *We shall overcome.*

Sources and References

Stories

A number of familiar myths, legends and stories are given in outline; the following list gives an indication of books in which they have been written up for reading or telling to children. Biographical sources are also indicated, so that teachers may build up their own narratives from such basic material.

A Wonderful World
Green, R. L., *Tales the Muses Told*, Bodley Head (Callisto).
Krall, B. C., *Stories of Favourite Saints*, REP (Bernard, Martin).
Martin, W. K., *The Concise British Flora in Colour*, Michael Joseph (Keble Martin).
Rose, M. E., *The Morning Cockerel Book of Readings*, Hart-Davis (Linnaeus).
Taylor, D. J., *The Senses–I*, Lutterworth Educational (Bentley).

My Neighbour
Bull, N. J., *Workers for God*, Hulton (Barnardo).
Hayes, E., *See His Banner Go*, REP (Stephenson).
Mattock, G., *Me—2*, Lutterworth Educational (Rahere).
Scott, C., *The Pilot Who Changed Course*, Lutterworth Educational (Cheshire).
Taylor, D. J., *Homes—1*, Lutterworth Educational (Pestalozzi).

Glad Days
Almedingen, E. M., *Francis of Assisi*, Bodley Head.
Johnson, L. S., *Happy Birthdays Round the World*, Odhams.
Rose, M. E., *The Morning Cockerel Book of Readings*, Hart-Davis (A Mexican birthday story).
Watson, J. W., *India: Old Land, New Nation*, Muller (Durga).

People with Courage
Bull, N. J., *The Early Saints*, Hulton (Ignatius).
Higgins, E. T., *Still Life*, Mowbrays.
Montgomerie, N., *More Stories to Read and to Tell*, Bodley Head (Gibbon, Masham).
Sperry, A., *The Boy Who Was Afraid*, Bodley Head.
Wilson, D. C., *Take My Hands*, Hodder (Verghese).

Festivals of Light
Cole, O., *World Religions in the Primary School*, C.E.M.
Frank, A., *The Diary of Anne Frank*, Vallentine.
H. C. Lefever, *One Man and His Dog*. Ancient Eastern Myths and Legends, Lutterworth Educational.
Living in a Multi-faith Society, C.E.M.
Robinson, H. S., and Wilson, K., *The Encyclopaedia of Myths and Legends of all nations*, Edmund Ward (Rama).
Sharpe, Eric J., *Thinking About Hinduism*, Lutterworth Educational.
Watson, J. W., *India: old land, new nation*, Muller (Divali).
Woodward, P., *World religions: aids for teachers*, Community Relations Commission.

People and Places
MacKinnon, C., *Stories of Courage*, Oxford (Darling).

A Story to Tell
The Wakefield Shepherds' play (Mak). A modern English version is given in D. Foye, *The Lamb and the Child*, Bodley Head (Mak).

Isn't He Clever!
Keats, E. J., *The Little Drummer Boy*, Bodley Head.
Kingsland, L. W. (trans.), *Hans Andersen's Fairy Tales*, Oxford.
Kossoff, D., *Bible Stories Retold*, Collins.
Manning-Sanders, R., *The Story of Hans Andersen*, Heinemann.
Rizzati, M. L., *The Life and Times of Michelangelo*, Hamlyn.
Rose M. E., *The Morning Cockerel Book of Readings*, Hart-Davis.
Winter, D., *New Singer: New Song*, Hodder (Richard).

Living with Danger
Bedford, J., *London's Burning*, Abelard Schumann (Great fire, 1666).
Fidler, K., *True Tales of Escape*, Lutterworth (Captain Neilson).
Hodges, C. W., *The Overland Launch*, G. Bell and Sons (The Lynmouth lifeboat).
RNLI, *The Lifeboat*, April 1971 (The picnic which lasted all night).

Looking Forward to Easter
Dale, A. T., *New World; the Heart of the New Testament in Plain English*, Oxford.

Think of a World without . . .
Andrist, R., *Heroes of Polar Exploration*, Cassell (Oates).
Martindale, A., *The Complete Paintings of Giotto*, Weidenfeld and Nicolson.
Warner, O., *Captain Cook and the South Pacific*, Cassell (Balboa).

It's Worth a Fight
Bull, N. J., *Workers for God*, Hulton (Ross).
Hogg, G., *Blind Jack of Knaresborough*, Phoenix House (Metcalf).
Peach, L. du G., *Florence Nightingale*, Ladybird.
Webster, G., *Journey into Light*, World's Work (Braille).
        The Guardian, 21.8.72 (Cornell).

Food, Glorious Food
Bull, N. J., *The Early Saints*, Hulton (Wilfrid).
Christian Aid, *Friends in Action*, folder 3 (Gaikwad).
Clark, J., *Food—1*, Lutterworth Educational.
Taylor, D. J., *Food—2*, Lutterworth Educational.

Trees
Allen, E., *The Latchkey Children*, Oxford.
BFBS, *The Birch Bark Talks*.

Follow my Leader
Martin, R. G., *Knight of the Snows*, Lutterworth.

Tales of Long Ago
Chaundler, C., *Everyman's Book of Legends*, Mowbrays (The Mexican myth).
Green, R. L., *Tales the Muses Told*, Bodley Head (Prometheus).

Achievement
Bannister, R., *First Four Minutes*, Putnam.
Hunt, J., *The Ascent of Everest*, Hodder.
Rose, M. E., *The Morning Cockerel Book of Readings*, Hart-Davis (Caedmon).
Unstead, R. J., *Great Leaders*, Black (Nuffield).

The Freedom Road
Mackinnon, C., *Stories of Courage*, Oxford (Aylward).
Petry, A., *The Girl Called Moses*, Methuen (Tubman).
Wymer, N., *Social Reformers*, Oxford (Shaftesbury).

Songs

No single collection of hymns meets all the needs of the Primary school and these suggestions deliberately refer to several sources. References are not given for traditional hymns which appear in the standard collections unless particular wording is advised.

Bailey, J., *New Life*, Galliard.
    Lord, I love to stamp and shout
    Now join we to praise the Creator

Bennett, G., and Tearnan, J., *Hello World*, Galliard.
    Lights go up at night in the city
    Mary set out on a winter's night

Brace, G., *Something to Sing at Assembly*, Cambridge.
    Gentle Christ, wise and good
    Up my neighbour
    We must help the poor and needy

Foote, G., *Merry Christmas*, Oxford.
    Silent night
    We wish you a merry Christmas

Oswin, Sister Mary, *Let God's Children Sing*, Geoffrey Chapman.
    Here comes Jesus riding on a donkey
    Martha and Mary

    Sing, Children of the Day, Geoffrey Chapman.
    The world was in darkness
    There on the hill a man is dying

Rose, M. E. and Cook, M. R., *The Morning Cockerel Hymn Book*, Hart-Davis.
    All things which live below the sky
    It fell upon a summer's day
    Like a great river flow the people
    Sing a glad song to Christ the King
    The lights go up all over the town
    To God who makes all lovely things

    When lamps are lighted in the town
    When oats and corn have ripened
    When puddles freeze in the glittering lane

Smith, P., *Faith, Folk and Clarity*, Galliard.
    Go down Moses
    Kum ba yah
    Thank you for every new good morning
    We shall overcome

Swann, D., *Sing Round the Year*, Bodley Head.
    The combines have lumbered through fields of wheat

Wyatt, E., and Ogden, B., *Sing to the King*, Church Army.
    Thank you for waking me this morning

Songs for the Seventies, Galliard and St. Andrew Press.
    Fisherman Peter on the sea
    Our Father, who art in heaven
    Think of a world without any flowers
    When I needed a neighbour

The School Assembly Book, Denholm House Press.
    Come let us remember the joys of the town
    For all the strength we have
    I sing a song of the saints of God
    We thank you, Lord of heaven.

Other sources
Davis, K., Onorati, H., Simeone, H., *The Little Drummer Boy*, Mills Music Inc.
Stanford, C. V., Shaw, G., *The New National Song Book*, Boosey and Hawkes
    (Sweet Polly Oliver).

Poems

The books quoted are those which are most likely to be known to teachers in schools rather than the original sources. Many of the poems appear in more than one collection.

A Wonderful World
Snow by Walter de la Mare, in *Collected Rhymes and Verses*, Faber.
The Snowflake by Walter de la Mare, in *Collected Rhymes and Verses*, Faber.
Snow Toward Evening by Melville Cane, in J. Britton (ed.), *An Anthology of Verse for Children*, 3, Oxford.

People and Places
The Thrush's Nest by John Clare, in E. Mears (ed.), *Mood and Rhythm III*, A. and C. Black.
We Thank You by L. E. Cox, in J. M. MacBain (ed.), *The Book of a Thousand Poems*, Evans.

A Story to Tell
The Donkey's Owner by Clive Sansom, in J. Gibson (ed.), *Poetry and Song II*, Macmillan.

Isn't He Clever
The Mother's Tale by Eleanor Farjeon, in *Silver-sand and Snow*, Michael Joseph.

Living with Danger
The Diver by W. W. E. Ross, in J. Britton (ed.), *An Anthology of Verse for Children*, 4, Oxford.

Looking Forward to Easter
The World Itself Keeps Easter Day by J. M. Neale, in L. Clark (ed.) *Common Ground*, Faber.

Think of a World without . . .
What is Pink? by Christina Rossetti, in J. Britton (ed.), *An Anthology of Verse for Children*, 1, Oxford.
A Thanksgiving to God for his House by Robert Herrick, in J. Britton (ed.), *An Anthology of Verse for Children*, 4, Oxford.

Trees
A Child's Song in Spring by E. Nesbit, in J. M. MacBain (ed.), *The Book of a Thousand Poems*, Evans.
Trees by Walter de la Mare, in J. Britton (ed.), *An Anthology of Verse for Children*, 4, Oxford.
Trees by Sara Coleridge, in J. M. MacBain (ed.), *The Book of a Thousand Poems*, Evans.
Loveliest of Trees by A. E. Housman, in E. Graham (ed.), *A Puffin Book of Verse*, Puffin.

Tales of Long Ago
Daffodils by William Wordsworth, in E. Mears (ed.), *Mood and Rhythm IV*, A. and C. Black.

Achievement
Hiawatha's Friends by H. W. Longfellow, in E. Mears (ed.), *Mood and Rhythm II*, A. and C. Black.

The Freedom Road
The Cry of the Children by Elizabeth Barrett Browning, in L. Clark (ed.), *Flutes and Cymbals*, Bodley Head.

Audio-visual Aids

Many pop records have a short life, so suggestions from this range are not listed, but the teacher whose ear is tuned to the radio will find current material to substitute for the given 'classics', if he wishes. Although a number is given for the classical records, teachers may have alternative recordings which are just as suitable. Short excerpts, only, should be used with children.

A Wonderful World

Film, *Animals in Winter*, Rank Films.
Film, *Children in Winter*, Rank Films.
Filmstrip, *The Seasons*, Society of St. Paul.
Record, *What a wonderful world*, Louis Armstrong, Probe GFF 106.

My Neighbour

Picture, *The Good Samaritan*, Paula Jordan, available from S.P.C.K.
Picture, *The Miracles and Parables of Jesus*, Benedictine Nuns of Cockfosters, Nelson.
Record, *Faith, Folk and Clarity*, Pilgrim JLP 148.

Glad Days

Record, *Bachianas Brasileiras*, no. 2, Villa-Lobos, HMV ALP 1603.

People with Courage

Picture, *Themes in Religious Education*, set 2, K. Smith, Macmillan.
Record, *Symphony in D minor*, op. 125, Beethoven, Phillips, GBL 5548.
Record, *Roman festivals*, Respighi, Supraphon 10364.

People and Places

Filmstrip, *Life on the Seashore*, Educational Productions.
Record, *Street Noises*, EMI 7FX 12.
Record, *Songs of British Birds*, HMV 7EG 8315.
Record, *Sounds of the Countryside*, RED 60M.
Record, *The Cockaigne Overture*, Elgar, Decca LXT 2525.

A Story to Tell
Picture, *Themes in Religious Education*, set 2, K. Smith, Macmillan.
Record, *Godspell*, MFP 5271.
Record, *Jesus Christ Superstar*, MFP 5280 or EMI Starline SRS 5125.
Record, *Procession of Palms*, Williamson, CLM 204.

Living with Danger
Record, *Sea Effects*, EMI 7FX6.
Record, *Four Sea Interludes: Peter Grimes*, Britten, Decca LXT 5564.

Looking Forward to Easter
Record, *Church bells*, EMI EFX 110.

Think of a World without. . . .
Pictures, *Home in Africa*, Oxfam.
Pictures, *Home in India*, Oxfam.
Poster, *Moon Walk*, Posters by Post.
Slides, *Men on the Moon. Apollo 15*, Woodmansterne.

It's Worth a Fight
Picture, *Themes in Religious Education*, set 2, K. Smith, Macmillan.
Poster, *Florence Nightingale*, Post Office Publicity Branch.

Food, Glorious Food
Pictures, *Help for Self Help*, FAO.
Pictures, *Hunger: Causes and Solutions*, Oxfam.
Poster, *Malnutrition*, SCF.
Record, *Oliver*, Bart, Decca LK 4359.
Record, *The Zemel choir: Israeli Songs*, MFR 1325.
Various, *India Resource Wallet*, Oxfam.

Follow my Leader
Slides, Grenfell Association.

Tales of Long Ago
Record, *Sounds of the Countryside*, RED 60M.

Achievement
Record, *Children's Corner Suite*, Debussy, Turnabout TV 341665.
Record, *The Story of Caedmon*, Scholey, A., and Swann, D., Galliard 4014.

The Freedom Road
Record, *Raisins and Almonds*, Marthe Schlamme, Fontana FJL 413.
Record, *We Shall Overcome*, Peter Seeger, BPG 62209.

Addresses

British and Foreign Bible Society, 146 Queen Victoria Street, London, EC4.
Christian Aid, 2 Sloane Gardens, London, SW1W 9BW.
Community Relations Commission, 10–12 Russell Square, London, WC1.
Commonwealth Institute, Kensington High Street, London W8 6NQ.
Dr. Barnardo's Homes, Tanner's Lane, Barkingside, Essex.
Freedom from Hunger Campaign, 17 Northumberland Avenue, London, WC2.
Grenfell Association, Hope House, 45 Great Peter Street, London, SW1.
Help the Aged, 8 Denman Street, London, W1A 2AP.
Mission for the Relief of Suffering, 7 Market Mews, London, W11.
National Children's Homes, 85 Highbury Park, London, N5.
Oxfam, 274 Banbury Road, Oxford, OX2 7DX.
Post Office Publicity Branch, London, EC1B 1HX.
Posters by Post, 43 Camden Passage, London, N1.
Robert Thompson's Craftsmen Ltd., Kilburn, Yorks.
Royal National Lifeboat Institution, 42 Grosvenor Gardens, London, SW1.
Save the Children Fund, 29 Queen Anne's Gate, London, SW1H 9DH.
S.P.C.K., 69 Great Peter Street, London, SW1.
Society of St. Paul, Langley, Slough, Bucks.
Voluntary Committee on Overseas Aid and Development, Education Unit, Parnell House, 25 Wilton Road, London, SW1V 1LY.
War on Want, 2B The Grove, Ealing, London, W5.
Woodmansterne Ltd., Holywell Industrial Estate, Watford, Herts.